STRINGSTASTIC

GRADE 2

2nd Edition

Suitable for any music examination board

By Lorraine Chai

STRINGSTASTIC

P.O. Box 815, Epping NSW 1710 Australia
www.stringstastic.com
Copyright © 2018 Lorraine Chai
2nd Edition 2021

Book design by Meilisa Lengkong

THE AUTHOR

Lorraine Chai
WORLD-CLASS COACH

Lorraine is a multi-talented instrumentalist, an international educator, and a world-class coach. She graduated from the Sydney Conservatorium of Music with a Bachelor of Music Studies in 2008 and completed her Graduate Diploma of Education at the Australian Catholic University a year later. Lorraine also holds a Postgraduate Diploma in Education from Birmingham City University.

Having grown up in a musical family, Lorraine began piano lessons at the age of four and violin at the age of six, giving her first violin performance at just seven years of age. Lorraine started teaching violin at the age of 14 and founded a string ensemble at her local church. From there, teaching and performing became her passion.

Lorraine loves finding new and exciting ways students can learn their instrument in a classroom setting as well as in private lessons. Along with her musical journey and exposure to the various educational methods including Kodaly, Suzuki, Orff, and Dalcroze, Lorraine has also attended Alexander Technique workshops and has found that she can integrate these various methods into her own teaching technique for the benefit of her students.

Lorraine has extensive ensemble and orchestral experience in Malaysia and in Australia. Lorraine is currently the Music Director of Stringstastic Pty Ltd and is the Vice President of Australian String Teachers Association, AUSTA NSW. She also co-ordinates instrumental programmes and runs string ensembles for some of Sydney's most celebrated schools.

PREFACE

Stringstastic Grade 2 follows on from the knowledge gained in Grade 1 and is specifically suited for violinists of all ages who are quick learners or who are interested in successfully completing music theory exams.

Every time you see these icons, these are what they mean

 *- NOTE/REMINDER*

 *- PLAY on your instrument*

For extra resources, go to www.stringstastic.com *to download them for free.*

Have fun!!

ACKNOWLEDGEMENT

This book was made possible with the encouragement of family and friends.
I would like to thank the following for their advice and input in making this book possible.

Dr. Rita Crews *OAM, FMusA (honoris causa), PhD(UNE), BA(Hons), AMusTCL, GradCertDistEd (UNE), FMusicolASMC, HonFNMSM, DipMus (honoris causa) (AICM) MIMT, MACE, MMTA, JP.*

Mary Nemet *AMusA, is a prominent string educator, AMEB Examiner, Reviews Editor for AUSTA Stringendo and contributor to Strings USA*

CONTENTS

Graded theory sample papers from different examination boards can be found on www.stringstastic.com.

Revision

Let us revise naming the notes on the treble clef. A reminder that we only use the first 7 letters of the alphabet. After G the note goes back to A.

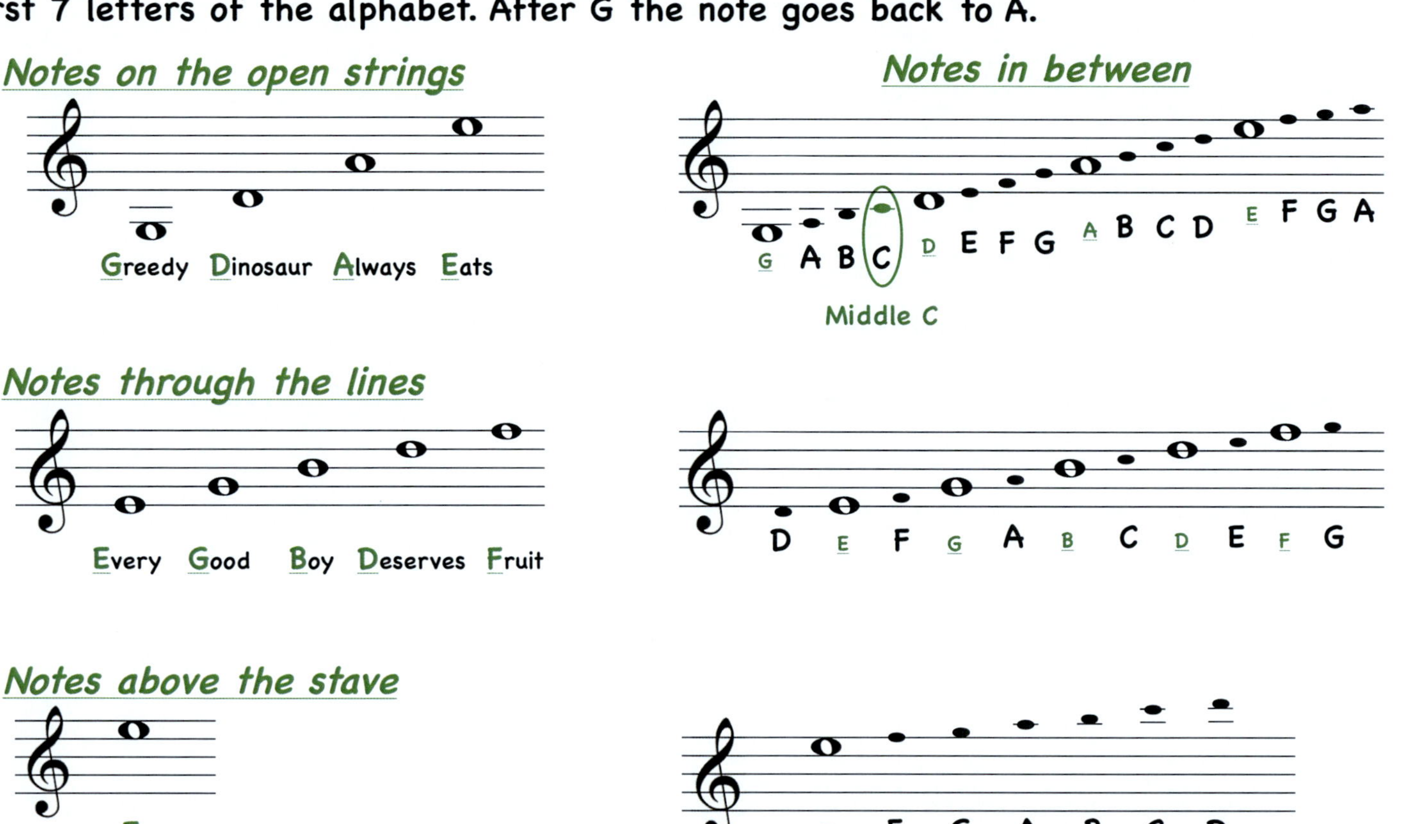

1. Name these notes without looking back to the top of the page. (Use capital letters.)

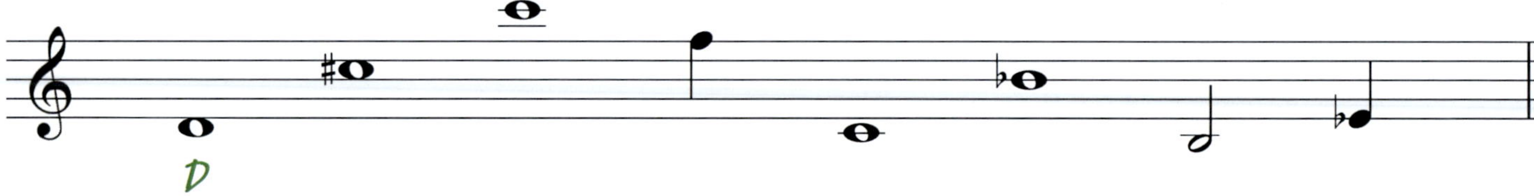

2. In semibreves, draw **THREE** different D flats.

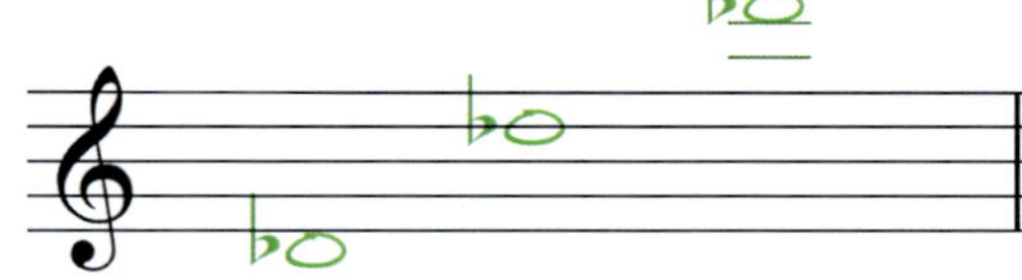

3. In minims, draw **THREE** different A sharps.

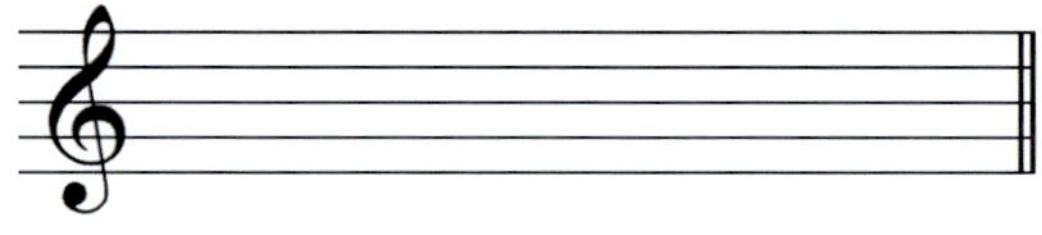

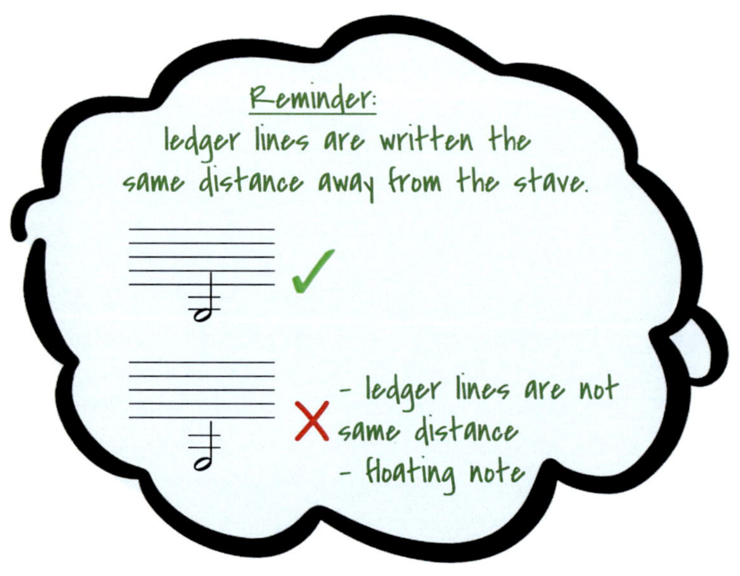

4

4. In semibreves, draw __THREE__ different B flats.

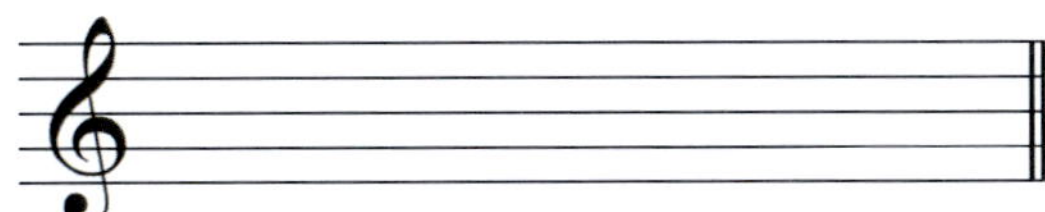

5. In minims, draw __THREE__ different A flats.

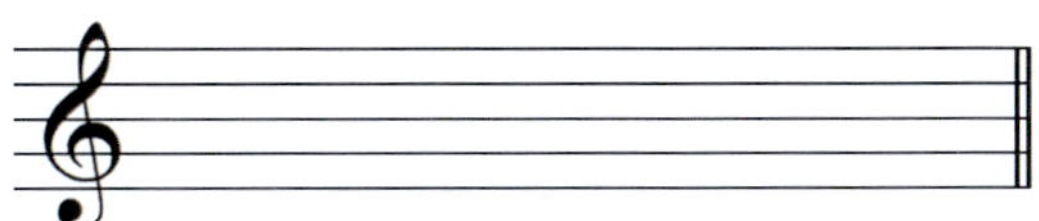

Now let us revise naming the notes on the bass clef. A reminder that we only use the first 7 letters of the alphabet.

Notes in the spaces

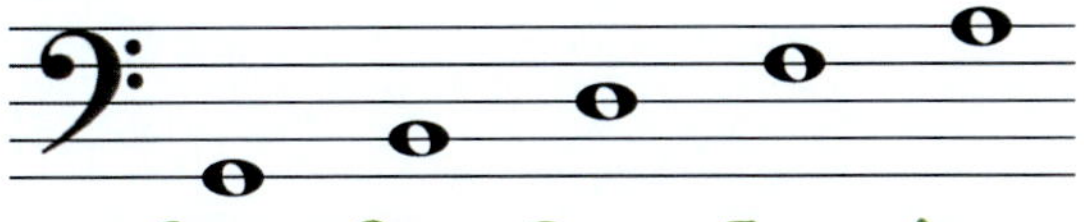

Notes above the stave

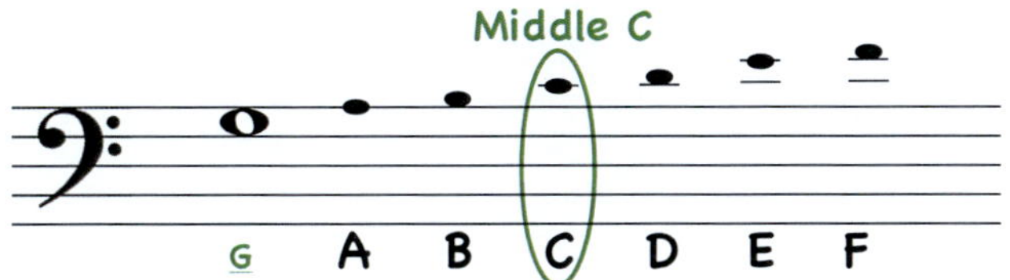

Notes below the stave

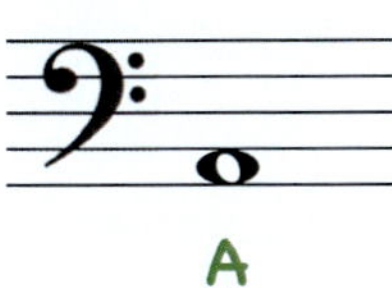

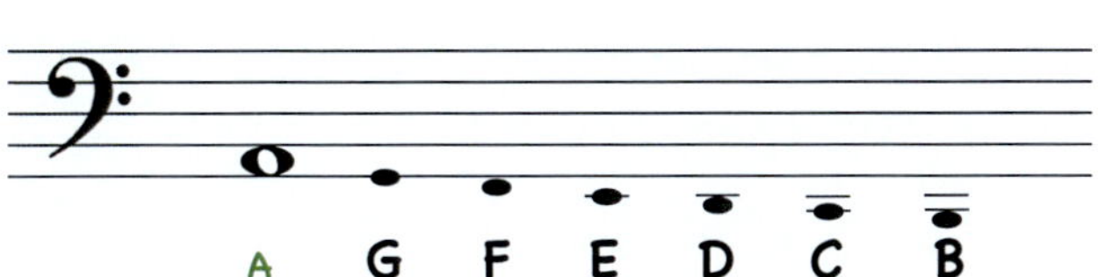

6. Name these notes without looking back to the top of the page. (Use capital letters.)

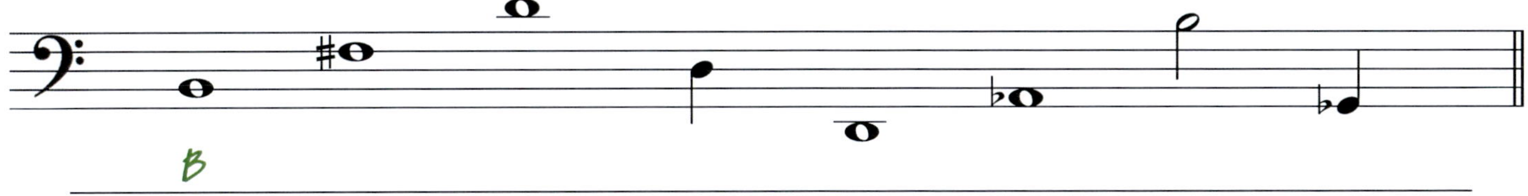

7. In semibreves, draw __THREE__ different C sharps.

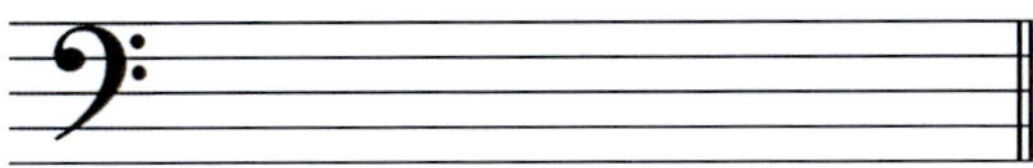

8. In minims, draw __THREE__ different E flats.

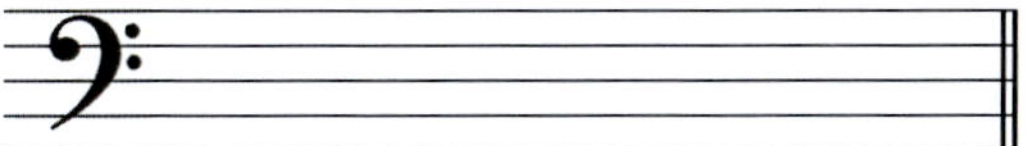

9. In crotchets, draw __THREE__ different C naturals.

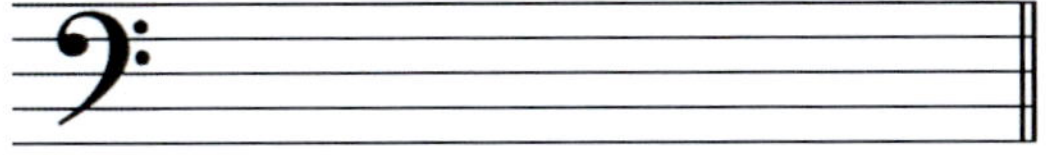

10. In minims, draw __THREE__ different B flats.

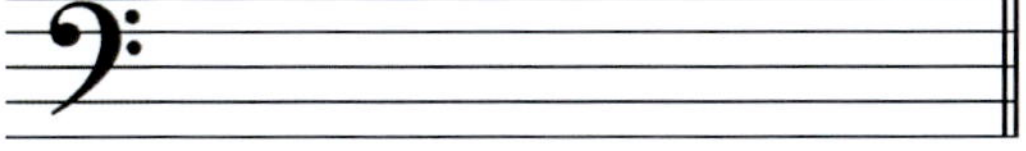

5

11. The following music contains <u>5 mistakes</u>. Circle the mistakes and write it out correctly.

Gustav Holst

12. Write in the correct beats and time signatures.

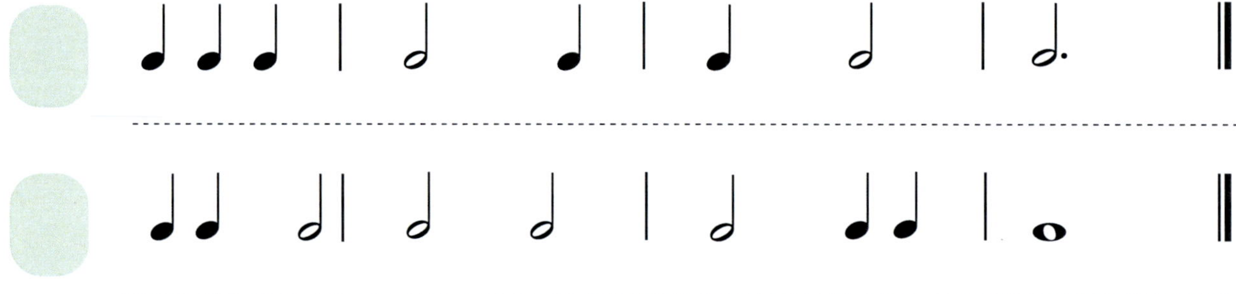

13. Name the interval and state if they are a harmonic or melodic interval.

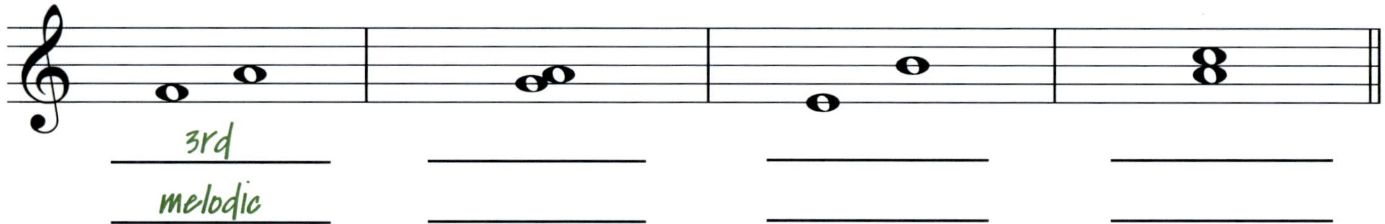

14. Write the scale of G major. (Take note of the clef.)
- Use accidentals
- Use semibreves
- One octave in a descending order
- Mark the tones with a slur

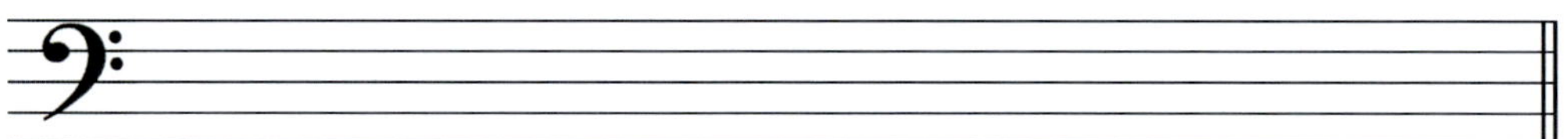

Note And Rest Values

In grade 2, we learn these new notes shown below.

NOTE	NOTE VALUE	NAME
♪	$^1/_2$	*Quaver*
♩.	$1\ ^1/_2$	*Dotted Crotchet*
𝅘𝅥𝅯	$^1/_4$	*Semiquaver*
𝅘𝅥𝅯𝅘𝅥𝅯𝅘𝅥𝅯𝅘𝅥𝅯	1	*Semiquavers*

1. <u>Figuring out the dot value.</u>

𝅗𝅥. = The note itself + $^1/_2$ value of itself

𝅗𝅥 + $^1/_2$ 𝅗𝅥

2 + 1 = 3 #

♩. = ♩ + $^1/_2$ ♩

1 + $^1/_2$ = $1^1/_2$ #

The dot next to the note means $^1/_2$ the value of itself.

2. <u>Quaver note value.</u>

1 quaver = $^1/_2$ count

2 quavers = 1 count

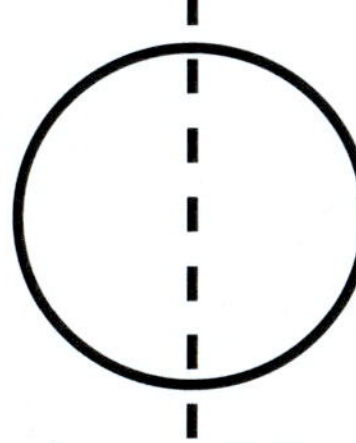

Think of quavers like a cake or a circle cut in half. When you join the 2 halves back together, it becomes 1 full circle.
When you add 2 quavers together, their total value is 1 count.

1. How many quavers beats do these notes need to create the same value?

𝅗𝅥	4
♩	

𝅝	
𝅗𝅥.	

2. How many crotchet beats do these notes need to create the same value?

♩	*2*
♪	

𝅝	
♩.	

---

3. **Semiquaver note value.**

A semiquaver note has 2 tails and is a smaller note value
then a quaver hence they are quicker notes.

1 semiquaver = $\frac{1}{4}$ count

2 semiquaver = $\frac{1}{2}$ count

4 semiquavers = 1 count

As you can see on the diagram on the right, we need 4 semiquaver notes to create a
whole note or a total value of 1 count.

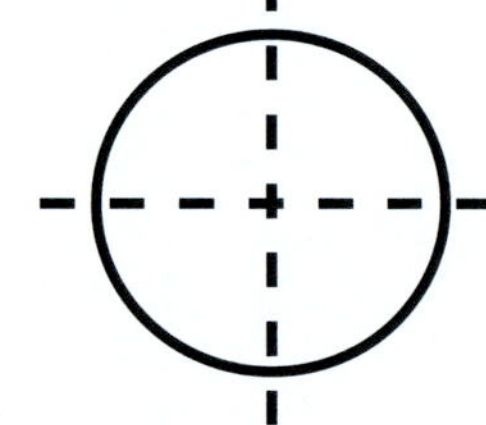

In grade 2, we only learn semiquaver notes which are beamed in groups of 4 to
create 1 crotchet beat.

---

3. Fill in the boxes with correctly grouped quavers to complete the bars.

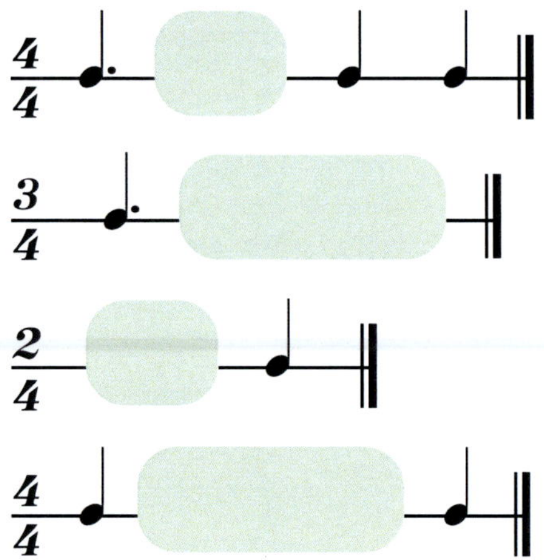

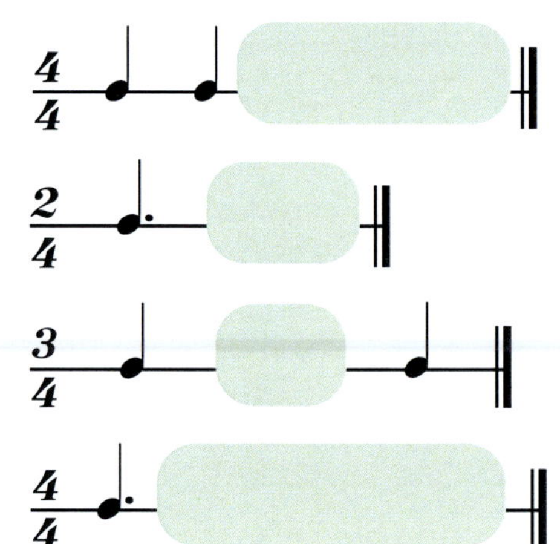

NOTE	REST	HOW IT LOOKS	NOTE VALUE	NAME
♪ tail	tail ♪	Number 7 starting with a dot	$\frac{1}{2}$	*Quaver Rest*
♬		F facing the left side	$\frac{1}{4}$	*Semiquaver Rest*

Below is a diagram which shows the number of notes of different lengths which is equal in value to a semibreve.

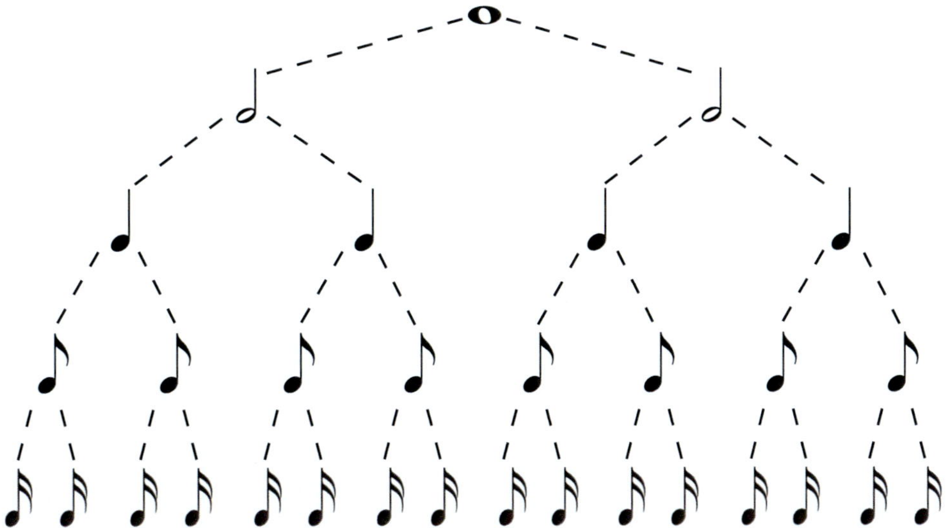

4. Answer the questions below.

a. How many crotchet beats are there in a semibreve? _______________________________

b. How many quaver beats are there in a minim? _______________________________

c. How many quaver beats are there in a semibreve? _______________________________

d. How many crotchet beats are there in a dotted minim? _______________________________

e. How many semiquaver beats are there in a quaver? _______________________________

f. How many quaver beats are there in a dotted crotchet? _______________________________

g. How many semiquaver beats are there in a dotted crotchet? _______________________

h. How many semiquaver beats are there in a minim? _______________________________

i. How many dotted crotchet beats are there in a dotted minim? _______________________

j. How many semiquaver beats are there in a semibreve? _______________________________

k. How many minim beats are there in a semibreve? _______________________________

l. How many semiquaver beats are there in a minim tied with a quaver? ________________

5. **Draw FOUR more quaver and semiquaver notes and rest.**

Quaver *(Tail is ALWAYS on the right side of the note.)*

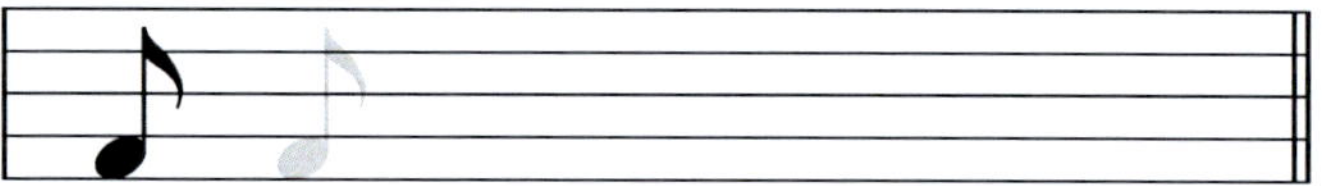

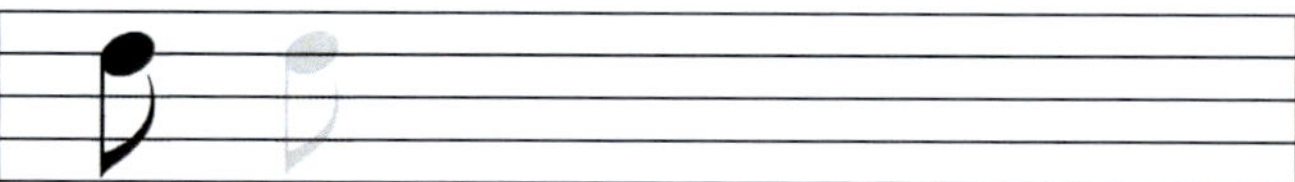

Semiquaver

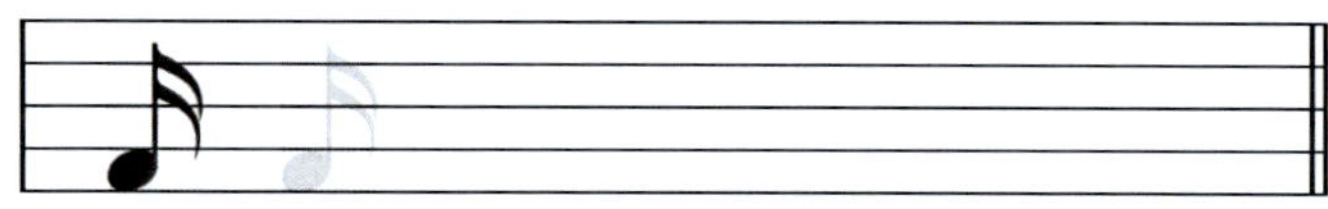

Semiquavers *(Draw 2 more sets.)*

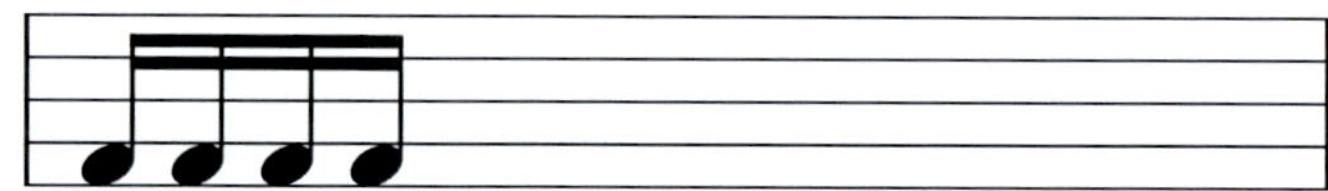

Quaver rest *(Start in the 4th space of the stave.)*
looks like a number 7 with a dot on the top

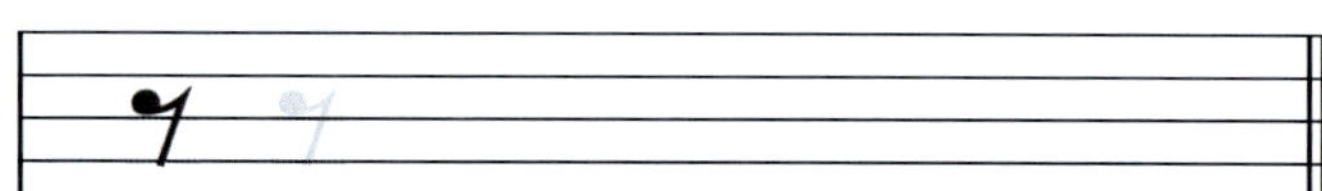

Semiquaver rest
(Start in the 4th space of the stave.)

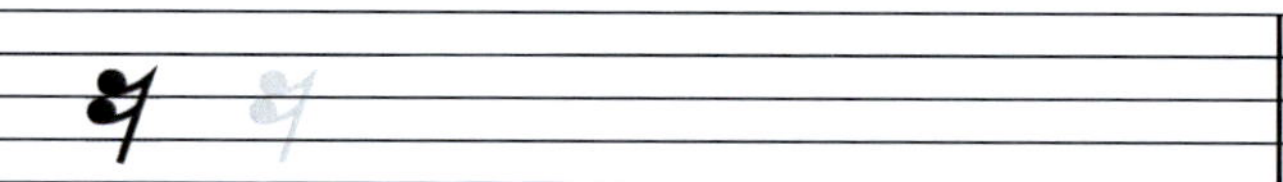

6. **Add the total number of crotchet beats of silence in these rests.**

	TOTAL
♪ 𝅗𝅥. ▬ ♫ ♪ 𝄽	4
𝄽 𝅗𝅥 ♪ ▬ ▬	
𝅗𝅥. ▬ 𝄽 ♪ ▬	
♪ ♪ ♪ ▬ ♬	
▬ 𝄽 𝅘𝅥 ▬ ♪ ♪ ♪	

7. **Fill in the boxes with correctly grouped rests to complete the bars.**

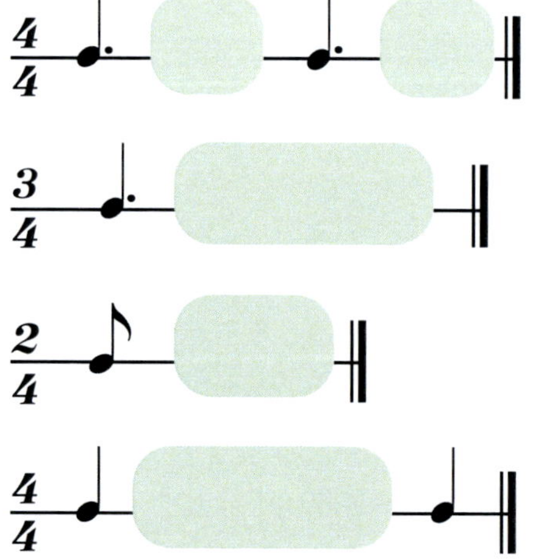

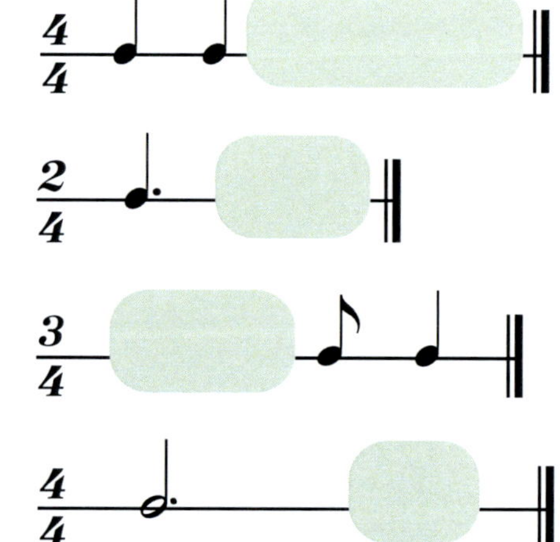

Triplet

A Triplet is a group of 3 notes played in the time of two notes.
It is identified by a number '*3*' written on the stem part of the note and is only used in <u>simple time signatures</u>. If there is no number 3, then it would not be considered as a triplet.

Every note can be divided into TWO equal beats. Below are just a few example.

Each beat can be divided into 3 equal parts which we call a triplet.

In grade 2, we will only be looking at the quaver triplets in crotchet beats.

When writing a '*3*' on the quavers, make sure it is over the beam of the quavers.

1. Circle the notes that are triplets.

2. Write in the correct time signature.

Time Signature

The time signature which we have learned so far has the number 4 at the bottom which shows that we should count in crotchet beats.

4 → number of beats per bar
4 → 4 = crotchet beats per bar

In the diagram on page 9, we see that we need 4 crotchet beats to make a semibreve, hence the bottom of the time signature is 4 which shows us that we should count each bar in crotchet beats.

In grade 2, we will learn to change the number on the bottom of the time signature.

1. $\frac{3}{8}$ → looking back on the diagram, we need 8 quavers to make a semibreve. Hence, __8 means quaver beats__.

$\frac{3}{8}$ means there are 3 quaver beats in each bar. In any quaver beat time signature, the quavers are grouped in THREEs and beamed together.

When using rests in $\frac{3}{8}$, use 2 quaver rests where there are 2 quaver beats of silence.

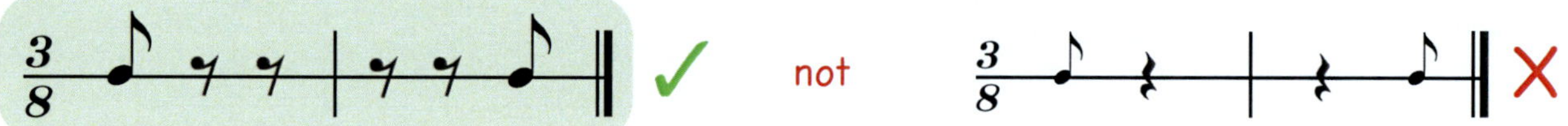

We do not have to use ties in this kind of time signature unless you are holding a note over the bar.

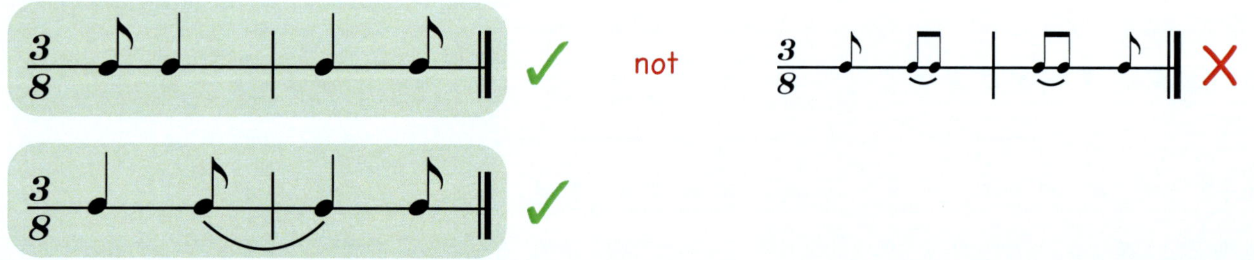

2.  looking back on the diagram, we need 2 minims to make a semibreve. Hence, **2 means minim beats**.

The note and rest grouping in this time signature is the same as the note grouping we have learnt in Grade 1 even though this is in minim beats.

 ✓ not 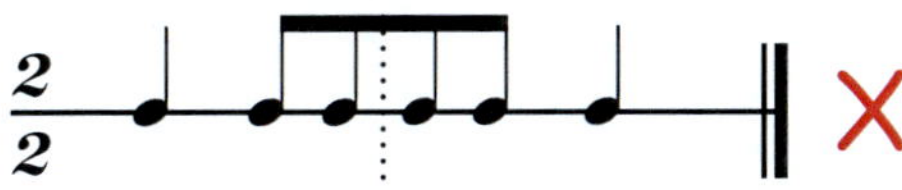 ✗

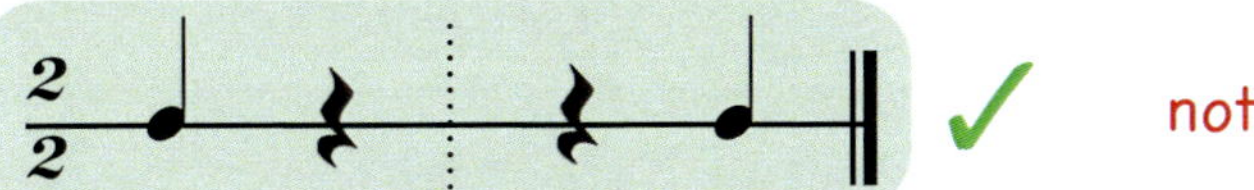 ✓ not 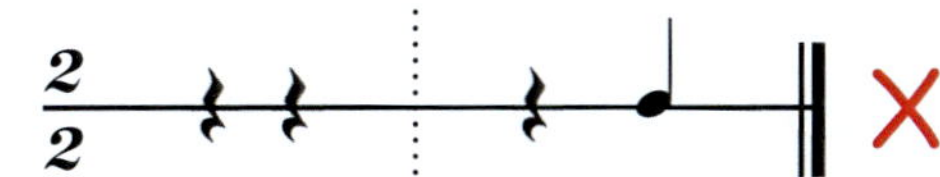 ✗

✓ not ✗

3. $\frac{3}{2}$

Like $\frac{2}{2}$, $\frac{3}{2}$ is also counted in minim beats. Notes and rests are grouped in minim beats.

A full bar's note in $\frac{3}{2}$ is 𝅝. *(includes the dot).*

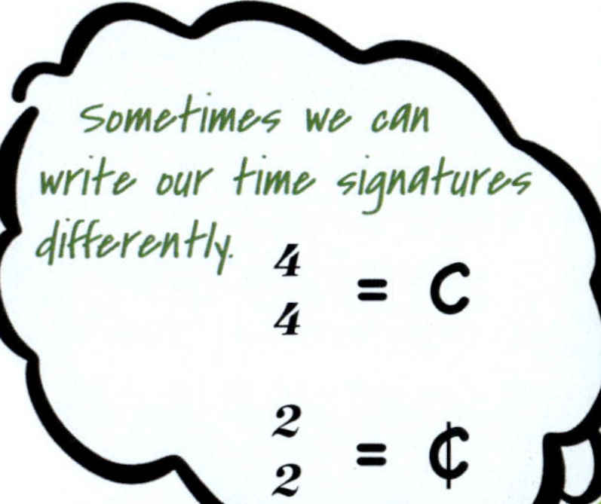

1. Fill in the boxes with the correct notes to complete the bars.

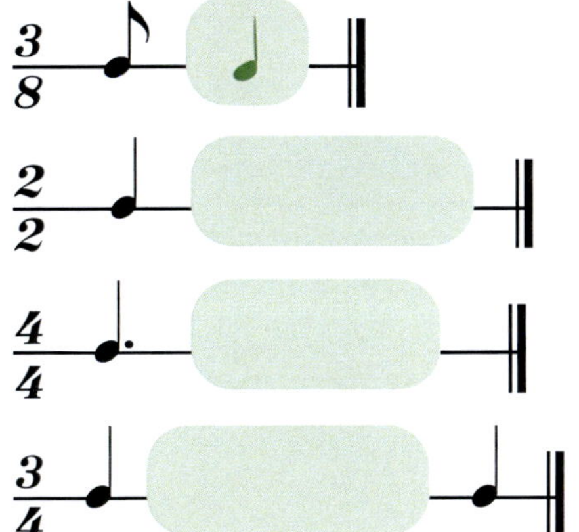

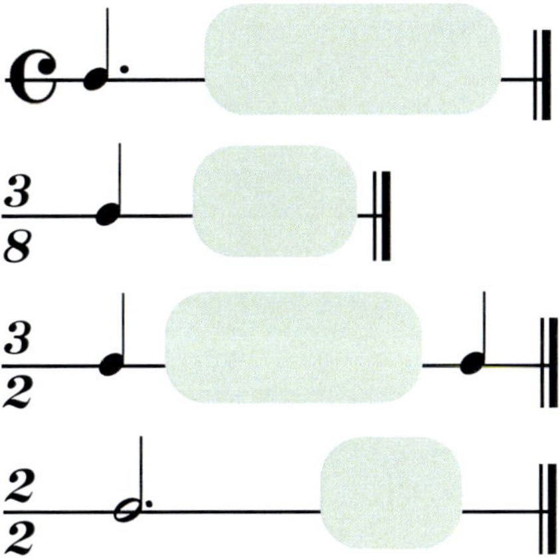

2. Fill in the boxes with correctly grouped rests to complete the bars.

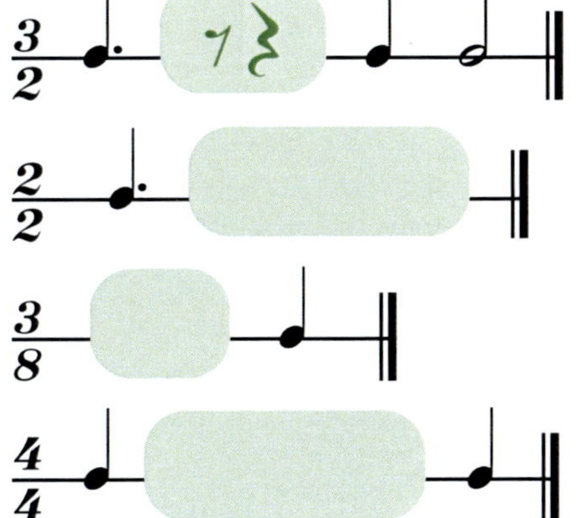

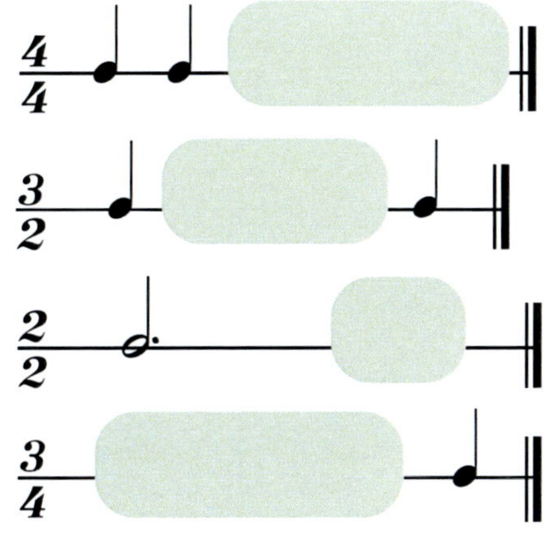

SIMPLE TIME	COMPOUND TIME
Simple and easier to count	More complex to count
Pulse can be divided into 2 beats	Pulse can be divided into 3 beats

	DUPLE	TRIPLE	QUADRUPLE
	2 beats per bar	3 beats per bar	4 beats per bar
SIMPLE TIME	$\frac{2}{2}$ $\frac{2}{4}$	$\frac{3}{2}$ $\frac{3}{4}$ $\frac{3}{8}$	$\frac{4}{4}$
COMPOUND TIME	$\frac{6}{8}$	$\frac{9}{8}$	$\frac{12}{8}$

3. Write out the correct number of beats. (Quavers, crotchets, minims.)

14

Slur Vs. Tie

Slurs and ties are curved lines joining 2 or more notes.

The line is drawn between the note heads ✓

between stems ✗

between note and stem ✗

They look the same, however their function varies.

SLUR	TIE

Notes sound and played SMOOTHLY	HOLD the note for the total amount of notes
Keep the bow moving in the same direction while changing your finger	Keep the bow moving in the same direction
Joined between DIFFERENT notes	Joined between 2 of the SAME notes

1. Identify if these curved lines are either a tie or slur.

slur

______________   ______________   ______________

______________   ______________   ______________

2. How many crotchet beats do you hold these notes for?

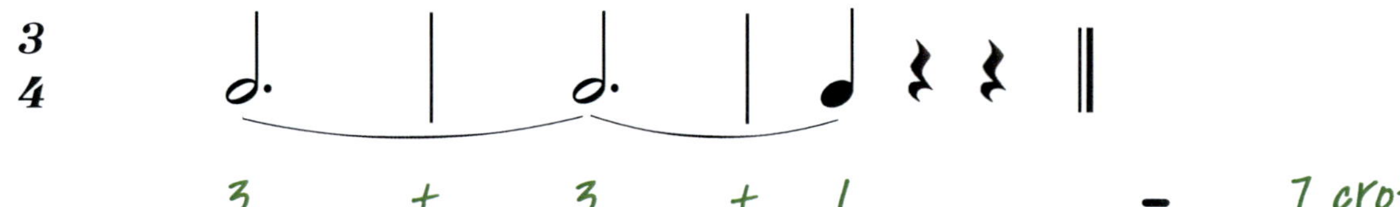

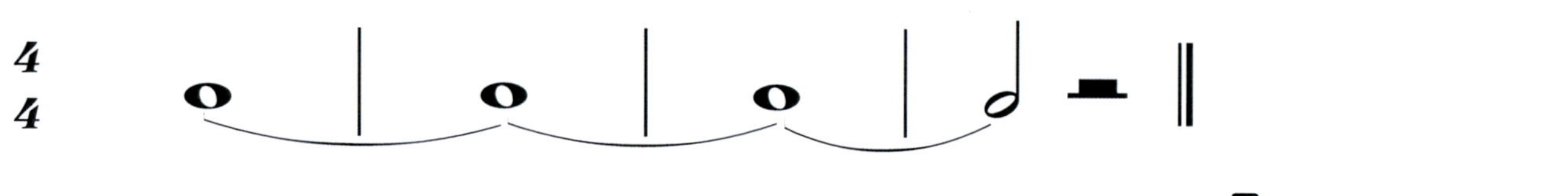

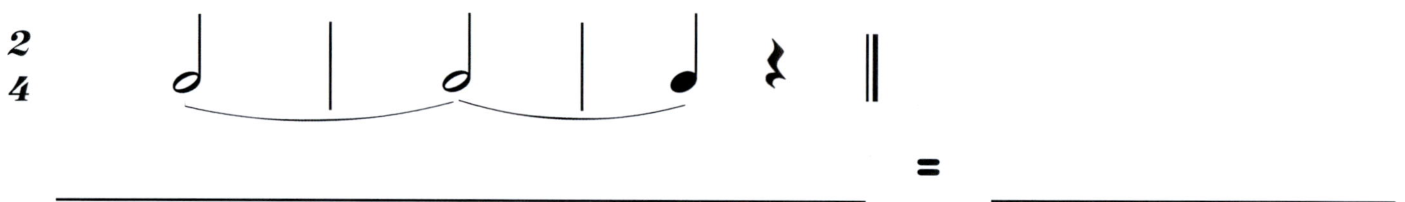

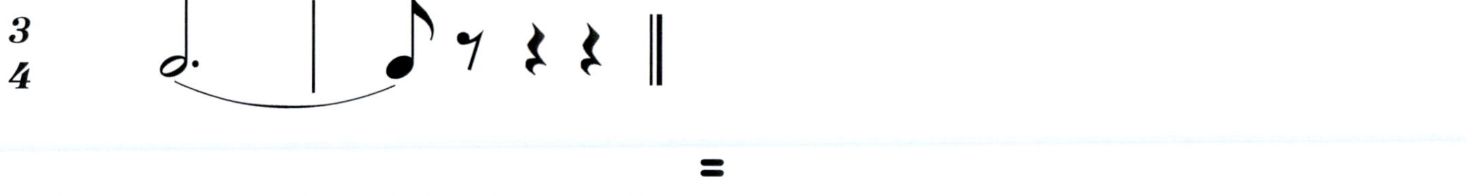

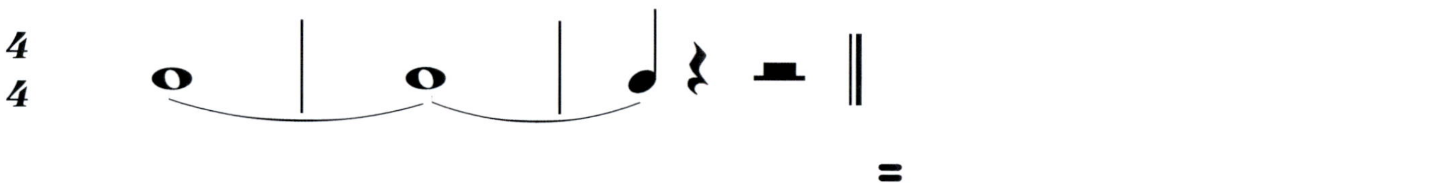

Syncopation

Syncopation is s shift of the normal beat. So instead of playing on the main beats, we play the notes **off beat** (between the beats).
This is another way of creating a different kind of rhythmic style in a composition.

Below are TWO syncopated patterns which you need to know in Grade 2.

1. Quaver as the first beat

off beat syncopation ➡

on the beat ➡

2. Crotchet as the first beat

off beat syncopation ➡

on the beat ➡

Think of syncopation where it breaks the rules of note grouping.

not

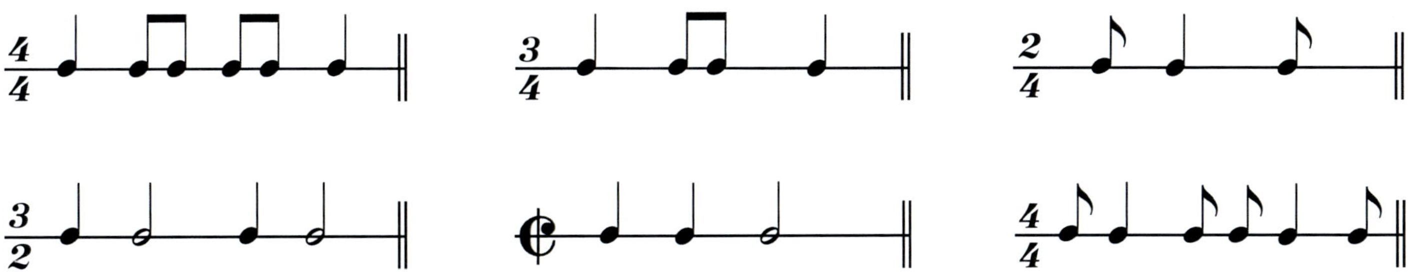

1. Below are different kinds of possible rhythm. Circle those showing syncopated rhythm.

2. Write TWO more repeats of these syncopated ostinati.

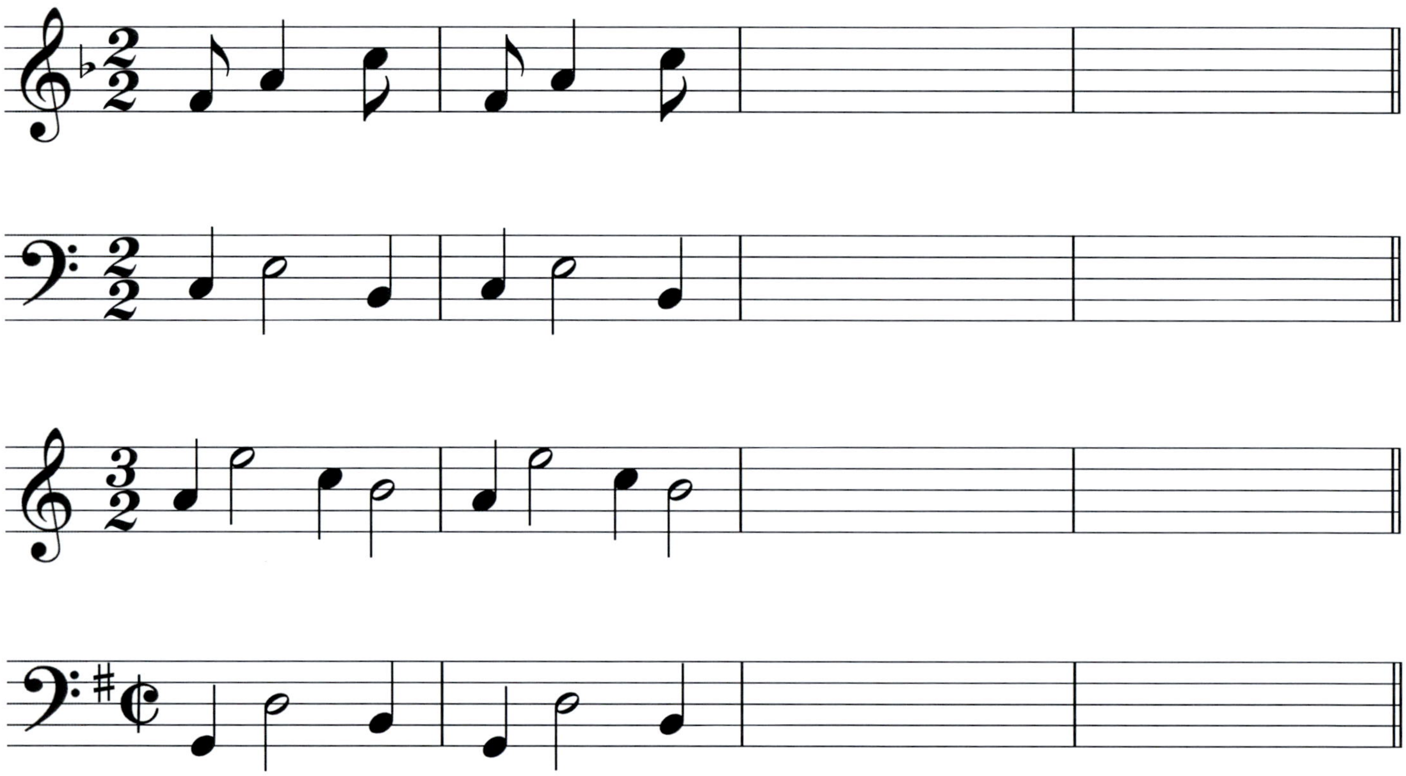

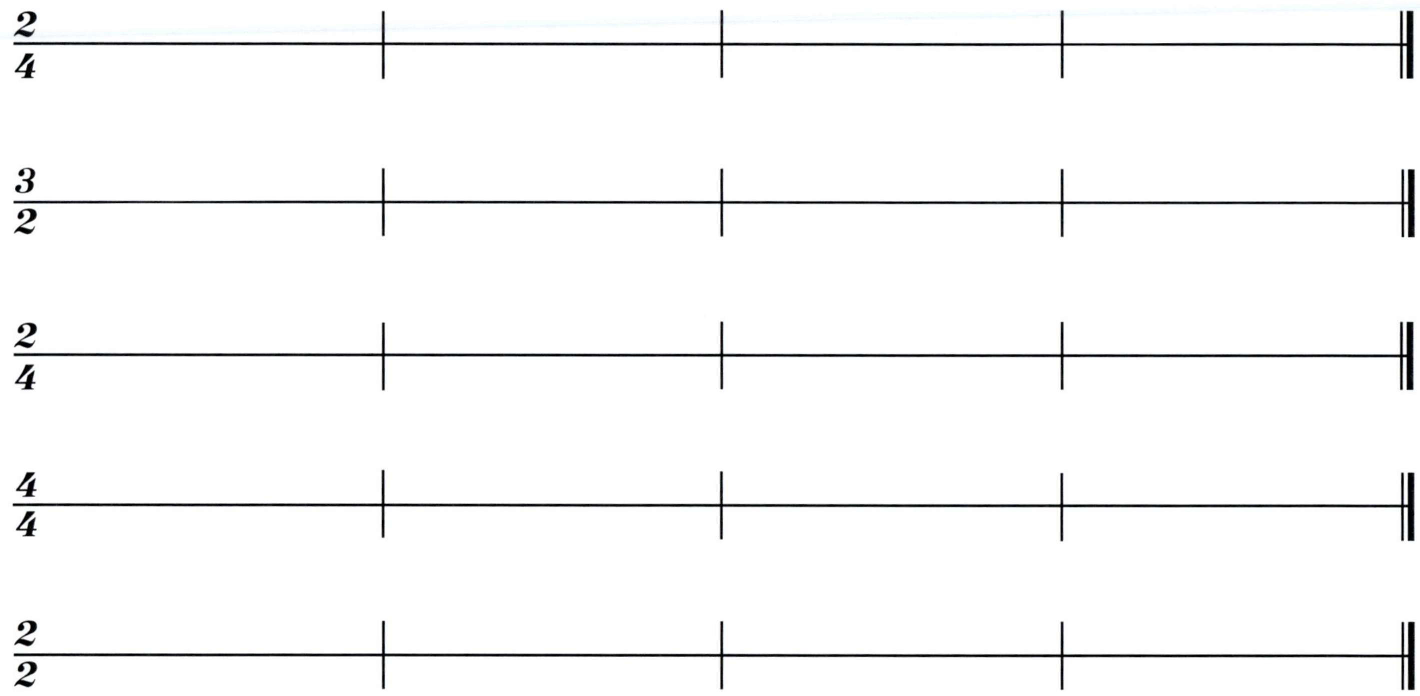

3. Write 4 bar rhythms using the note and rest values which you have learnt. Include at least THREE rests in every rhythm and ONE syncopated pattern.

What Have We Learnt So Far?

1. Name these notes.

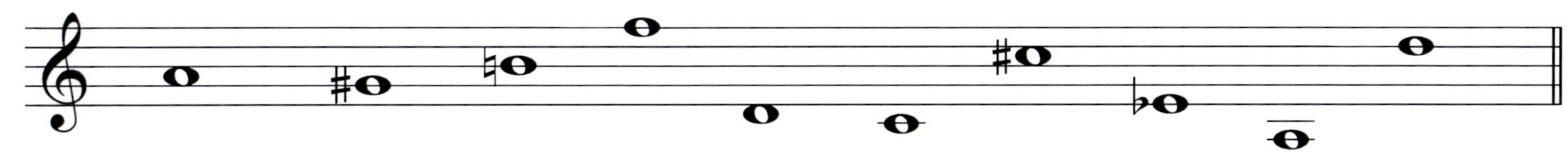

____

2. Label each note in question 1 with the correct fingering in the 1st position. (0, 1, 2, 3)

3. Draw these notes in the correct place.

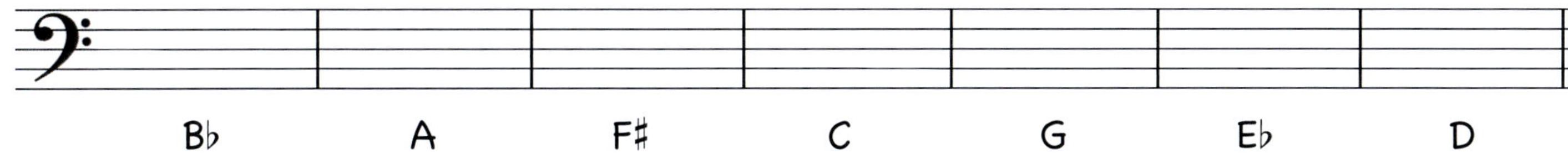

Bb   A   F#   C   G   Eb   D

4. Write in the correct time signature.

5. Write 4 bar rhythms using the note and rest values which you have learnt. Include at least __THREE__ rests in every rhythm.

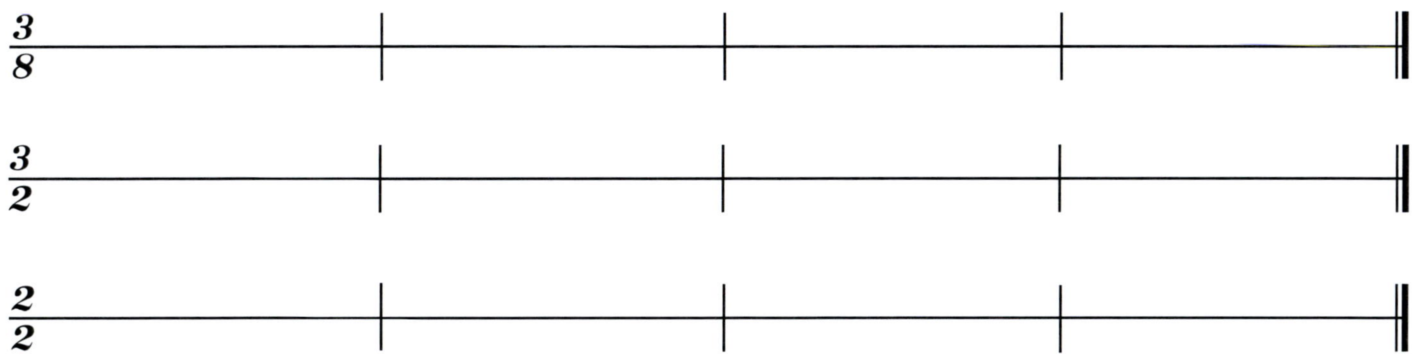

6. How many quaver beats are there in a dotted minim? _______________________

7. How many crotchet beats are there in a semibreve? _______________________

8. How many semiquaver beats are there in a dotted crotchet? _______________________

9. What does Vivace mean? _______________________

10. Add the total number of these rests.

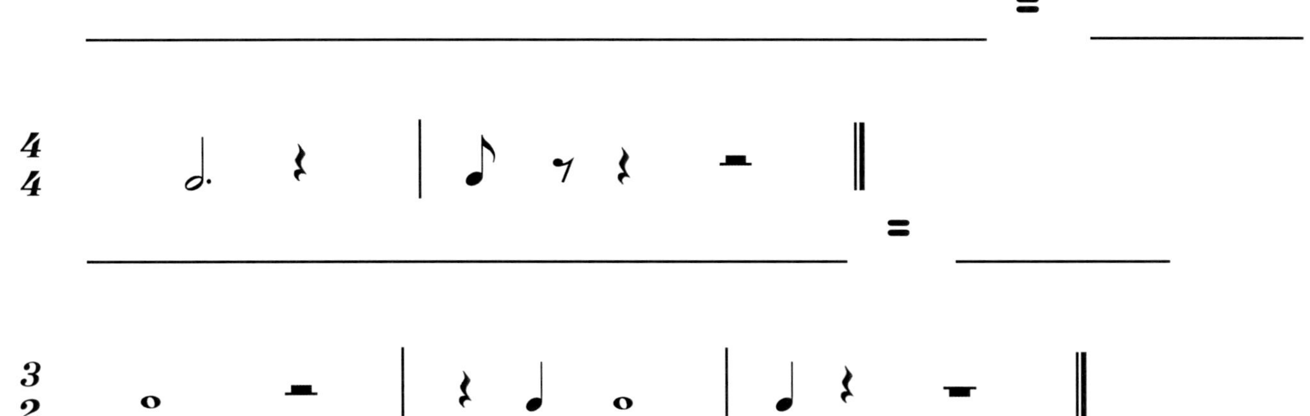

11. Fill in the boxes with correctly grouped notes to complete the bars.

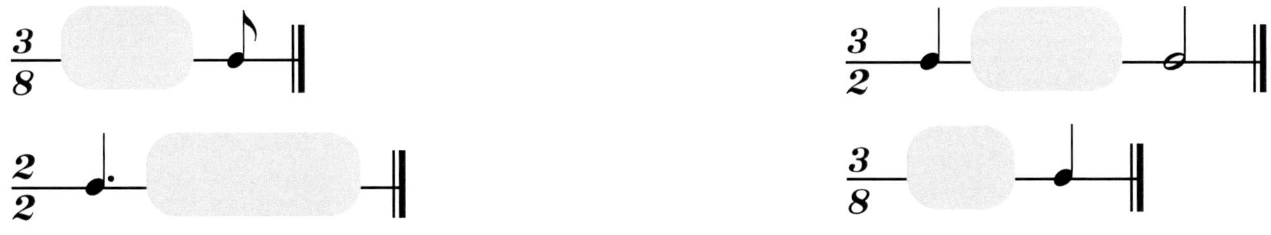

12. Fill in the boxes with correctly grouped rests to complete the bars.

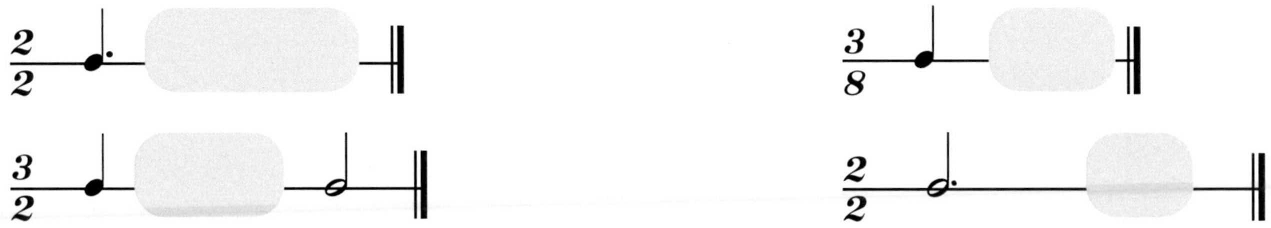

13.

	NAME THE LINE UNDER THE NOTES	HOW DO YOU PLAY THESE NOTES?

14. Write 4 bar rhythms using the note and rest values which you have learnt. Include <u>ONE</u> syncopated pattern.

Minor Scales

The difference between a major and minor scale is that major sounds happy and minor scales sound sad.

Major 
Minor

There are 3 different quality of minor scales.

MINOR
- natural
- harmonic
- melodic

It is very easy to remember the difference between the minor scales.

natural - normal (NO change)

Now look at the first letter of the next 2 minor scales.
How many humps/curves do they have?

harmonic - 1 hump/curve = 1 change
  raise the 7th note

melodic - 2 humps/curves = 2 changes
  raise the 6th & 7th notes going up ↑
  lower the 6th & 7th notes going down ↓

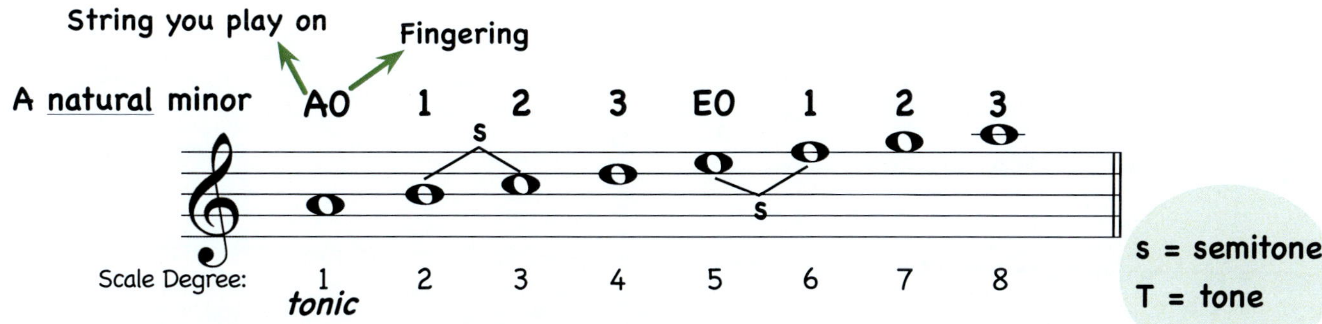

The tone-semitone pattern of any natural minor scale is as below,

$$T - s - T - T - s - T - T$$

1. Between which scale degree numbers are the semitones in a natural minor scale?

______-______ and ______-______

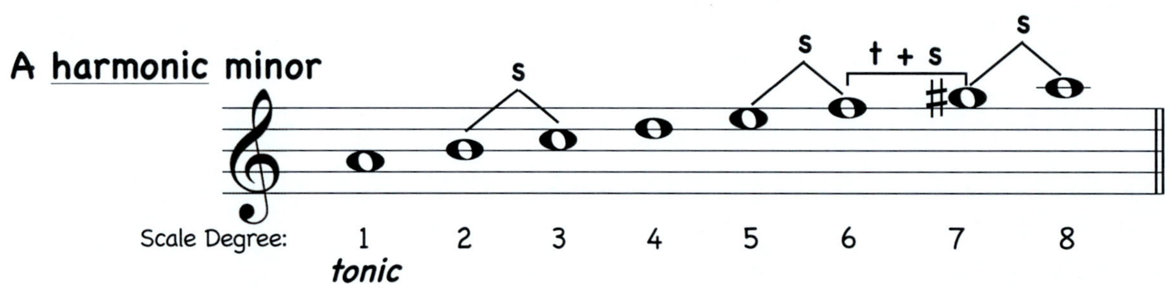

(There is always a (tone + semitone) pattern in a harmonic scale.)
6th & 7th degrees

The tone-semitone pattern of any harmonic minor scale is as below,

T - s - T - T - s - T and a half - s

2. Between which scale degree numbers are the semitones in a harmonic minor scale?

_____-_____ , _____-_____ and _____-_____

3. Change these A natural minors into harmonic minors.

Raise the 7th degree.

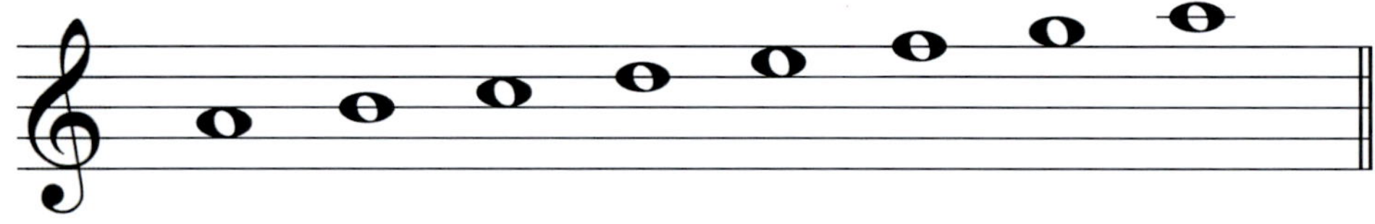

Count the scale degree from the lowest note.

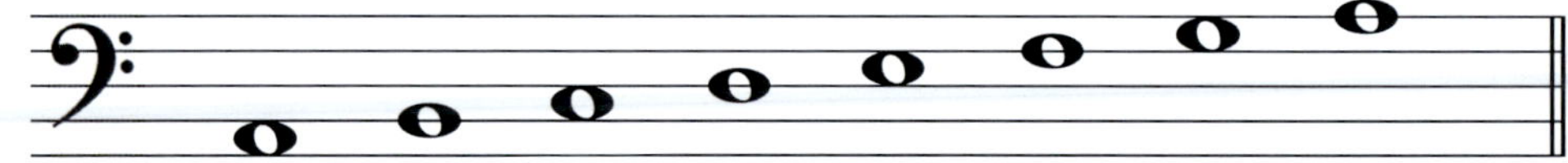

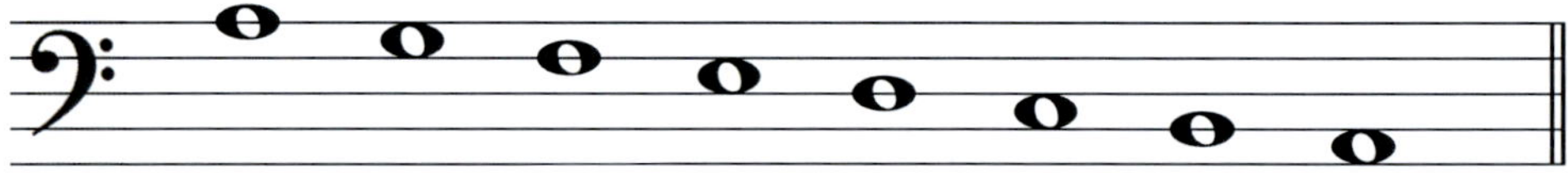

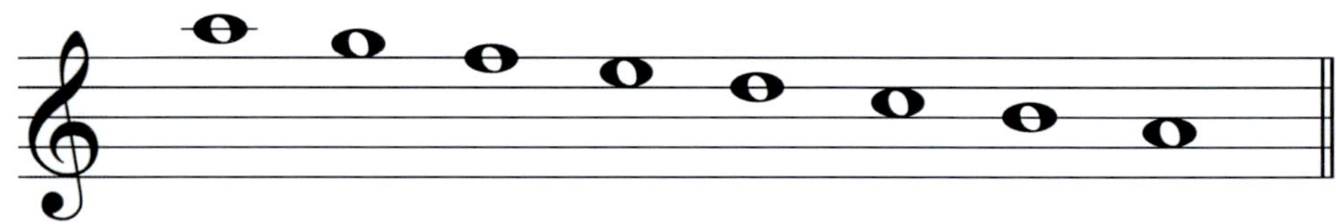

4. In first position, add the fingering on top of the notes on the treble clef in question 3.

22

For Grade 2, we only need to know about natural and harmonic minor scales.
However, for the curious mind, here is how a melodic minor scale looks.

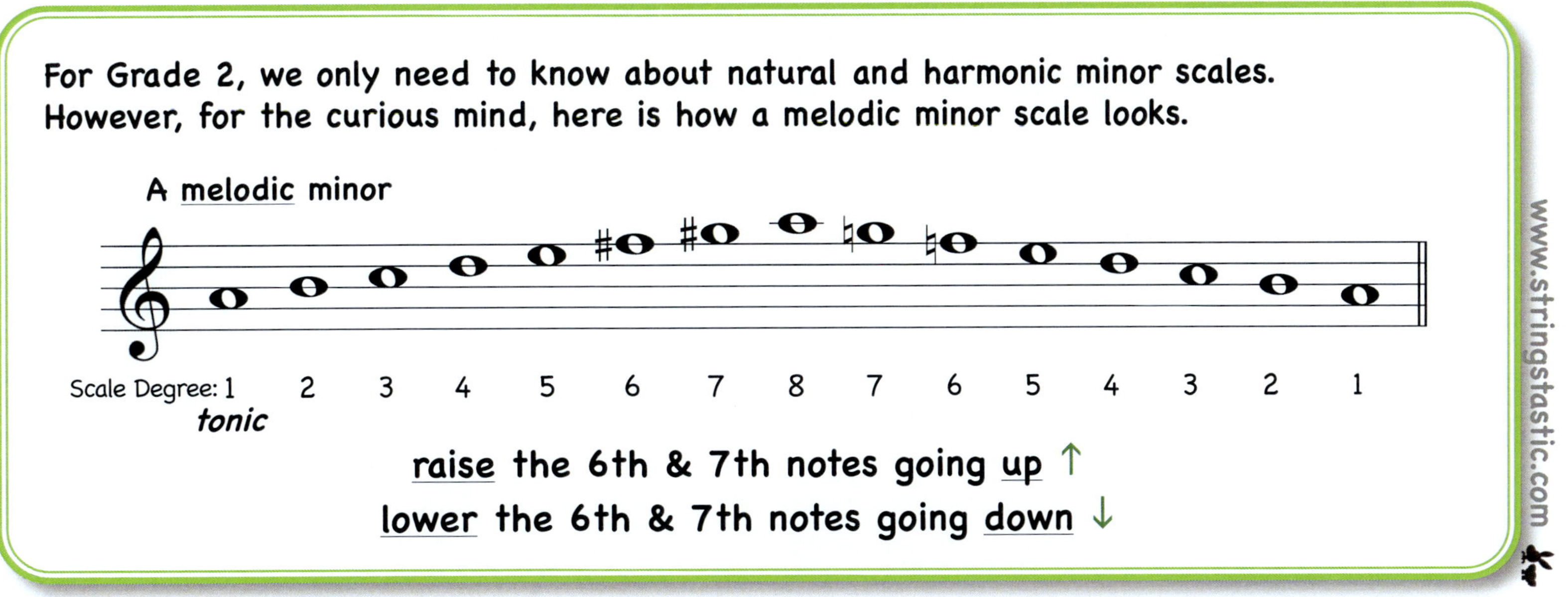

raise the 6th & 7th notes going **up** ↑

lower the 6th & 7th notes going **down** ↓

5. In minims, write a ONE octave minor scale in an ascending and descending order.
    Sometimes you need to add accidentals.

D harmonic minor

A harmonic minor

E natural minor

E harmonic minor

D natural minor

6. In first position, add the fingering on top of the notes in question 5.

Let us play all the scales in quesion 5.
Can you hear the difference between the different quality minor scales?

7. Now on the bass clef, write a ONE octave minor scale descending in minims.
The lowest note is scale degree 1.

D harmonic minor

A harmonic minor

E natural minor

E harmonic minor

D natural minor

8. On questions 3, 5, and 7, add slurs to show where the semitones are.

9. How many semitones are there in a harmonic minor scale? ______________________

10. On which scale degree in a harmonic minor scale would you find the two notes which

are a tone and a half? ______________________________

24

Minor Arpeggios

Remember from Grade 1, <u>arpeggios</u> are notes of a chord played one after another. We use the 1st, 3rd, and 5th notes of a scale. We also include the 8th note.

Eg.

A minor

A	B	C	D	E	F	G	A
1	2	3	4	5	6	7	8

1. Circle the notes of the arpeggio of these scales below.

   D minor

       D   E   F   G   A   B♭   C   D

   E minor

       E   F♯   G   A   B   C   D   E

2. Draw the notes of the arpeggio in an ascending and descending (going up then down) **order from these scales in semibreves.**

D minor

A minor

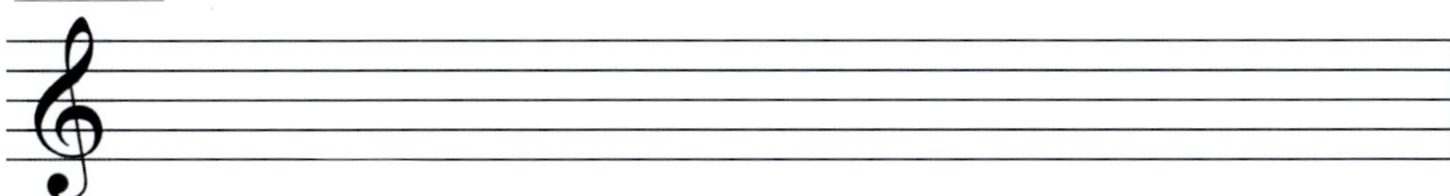

E minor

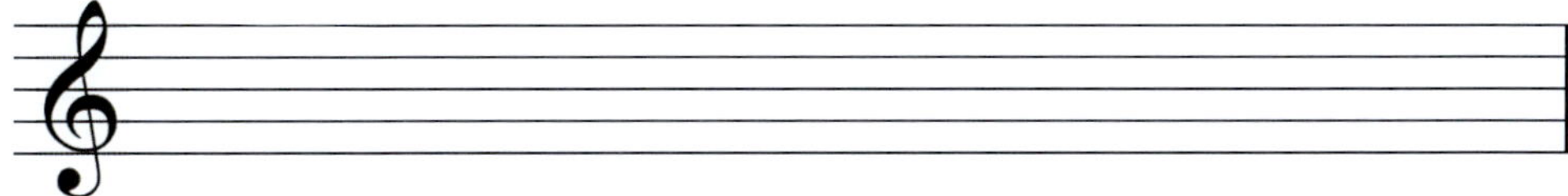

3. Add the fingering on top of the notes in question 2.

25

4. Draw the same scales ascending and its arpeggios on the right in crotchets.
Find the starting note.

A natural minor

D natural minor

E natural minor

5. Draw the same scales descending in the appropriate clef in minims.

A harmonic minor

D harmonic minor

E harmonic minor

6. Now draw the same scales in an ascending and descending order in the appropriate clef in semibreves.

A melodic minor

D melodic minor

E melodic minor

7. **Label the scales below. Then draw the other notes of the tonic triads and label them with Roman numerals.** (NOTE: Scales below are written with and without key signature.)

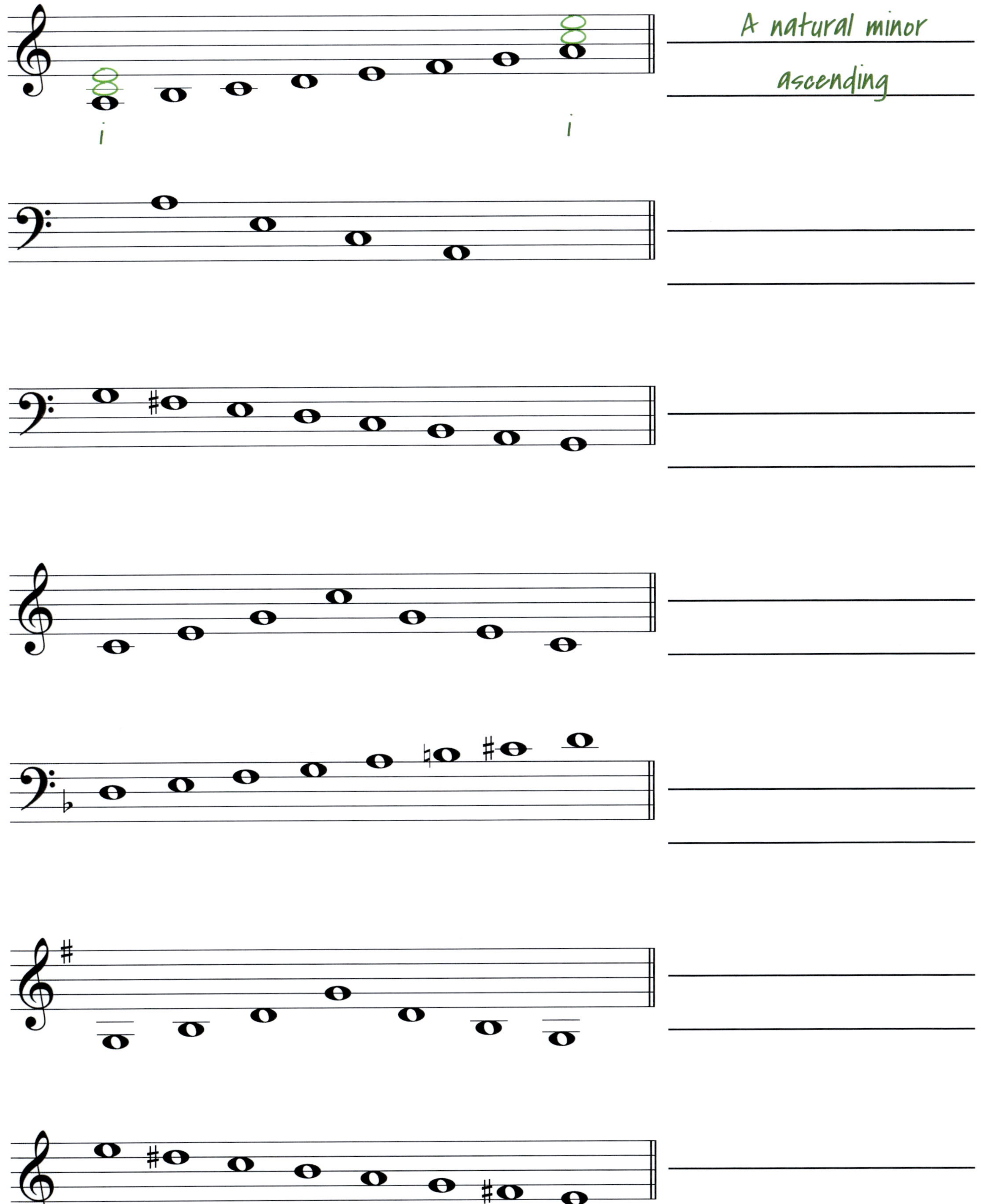

27

Relative Minors and Majors

Just as you have direct relatives in your family, major keys have minor keys who are relatives – think of it as your relatives that share the same surname as you do. The major and relative minors share the same key signature.

From Grade 1, we learnt that C major has no sharps or flats in its key signature. The related minor key to C major is A minor which means A minor also does not have any sharps or flats in its key signature.

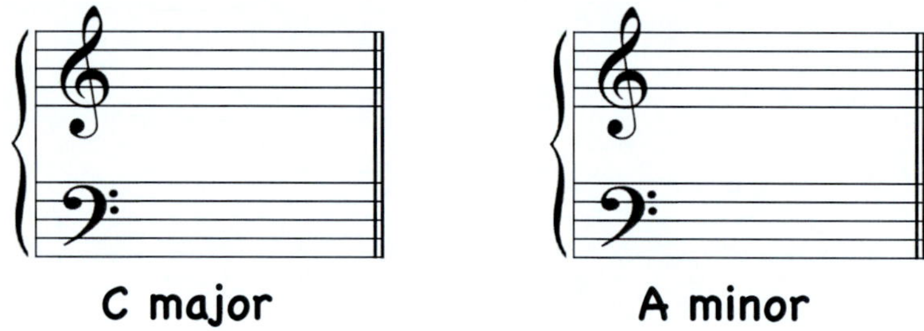

C major   A minor

Try and memorize that C major is related to A minor.

There are a few ways of finding out the relative minors of the major keys. Let us look at your fingeringboard in 1st position and find the note A and C.

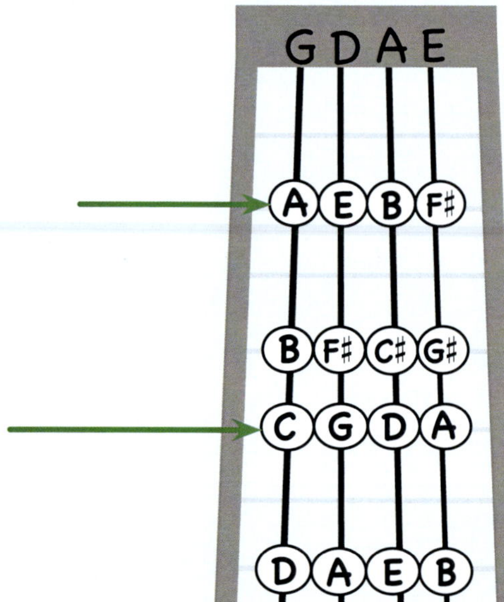

How many steps does it takes from the note C backwards to A?

 When counting the steps between notes in figuring out the relative minors or majors, always use and count the shortest distance between notes.

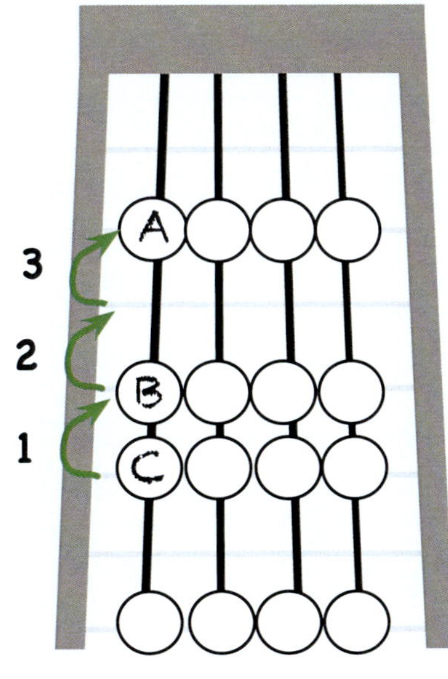

It only takes 3 steps back from C to A.

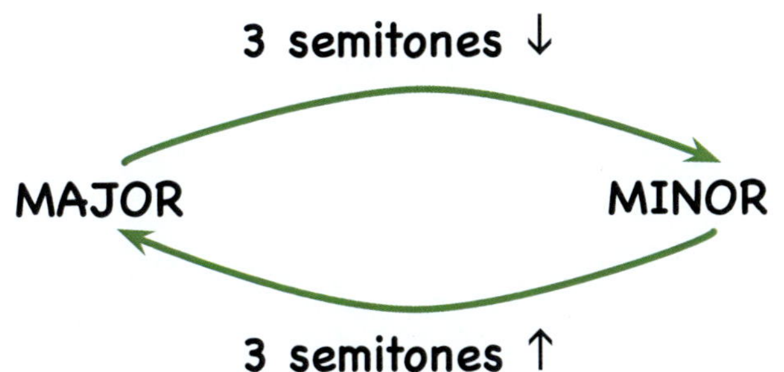

Hence the relative minors for the major scales we have learnt are.

C major ⟶ A minor

G major ⟶ E minor

F major ⟶ D minor

Check on the fingerboard in the previous page to see if the related minors for the major scales above are correct.

Below are how the key signature would look for each related key.

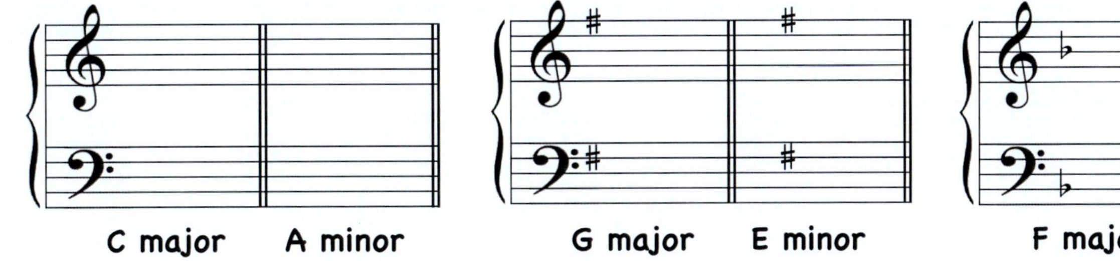

1. Fill in the blanks. Try not to look above.

MAJOR SCALE	RELATIVE MINOR	KEY SIGNATURE
C Major		–
F Major		B♭
G Major		

2. Draw the key signatures for each of these keys. (Take care with the clef.)

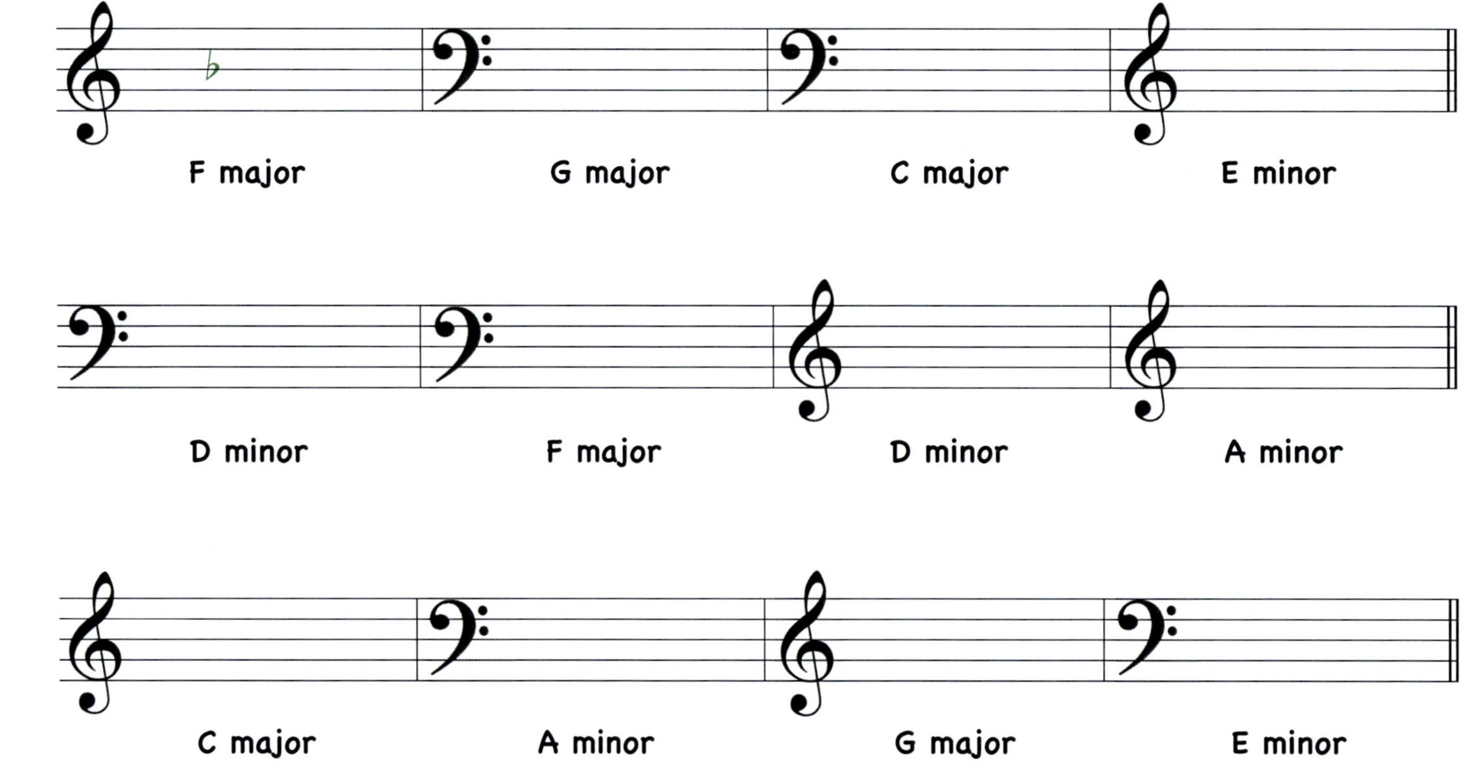

3. Now draw the tonic note in question 2 for each key. Be careful of the clef.

4. Find the tonic note and relative major key of each of these minor keys.
Count 3 semitones up.

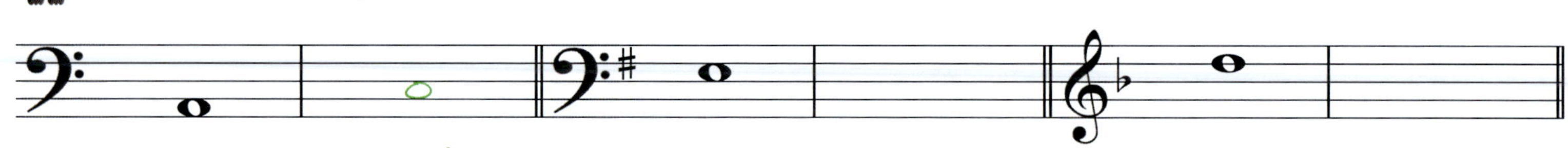

5. Find the tonic note and relative minor key of each of these major keys.
Count 3 semitones down.

Key Signature

Memorising key signatures assists us in understanding and memorising our scales. There are a few ways of memorising key signatures.

So far we already know the key signature for these scales.

C major – NO ♯s or ♭s

G major – F♯

1. Remember that SHARP is higher *(forward)* and FLAT is lower (backward). All we have to do is remember the first 2 scales in order and alternate the letters forwards.

Now let us look at how we can figure out key signatures with sharps.

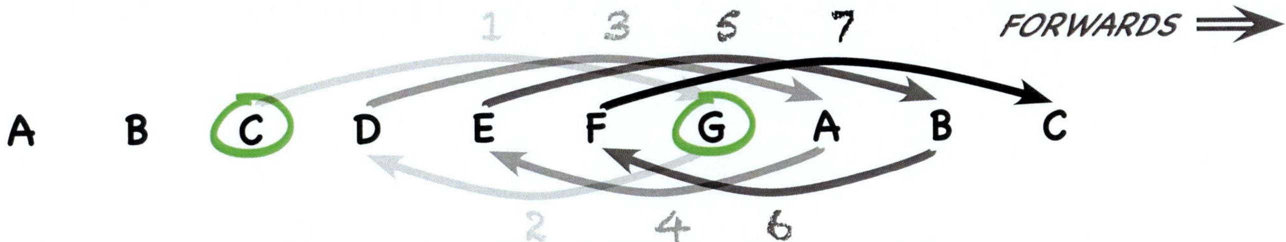

We ONLY need to remember F♯ and C♯ and alternate forward between the TWO to figure out the rest of the SHARPS.
F♯ and C♯ are the first 2 sharps we learnt so would be easy to remember.

We ONLY need to remember C and G and alternate forward between the TWO to figure out the rest in order.

NO.	SHARPS	SCALE
0	–	C major
1	F♯	G major
2	F♯, C♯	D major
3	F♯, C♯, G♯	A major
4	F♯, C♯, G♯, D♯	E major
5	F♯, C♯, G♯, D♯, A♯	B major
6	F♯, C♯, G♯, D♯, A♯, E♯	F♯ major
7	F♯, C♯, G♯, D♯, A♯, E♯, B♯	C♯ major

They cannot be F major or C major as F major has a flat and C major has NO flats or sharps

Same thing as figuring out the sharps. All you have to remember is F♯ and C♯. Then **alternate** them *forward* to figure out the rest.

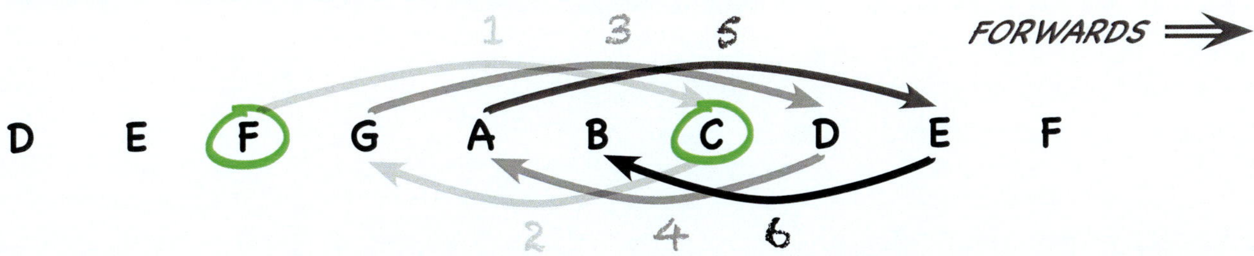

You can figure out the key signature this way or by using the Circle of 5ths as shown on the diagram on the next page. Start on C and count forward by 5 each time. The same thing on figuring out the sharps.

Now let us look at how we can figure out key signatures with flats.
Remember that flats are lower hence <u>alternate</u> the letters backwards.

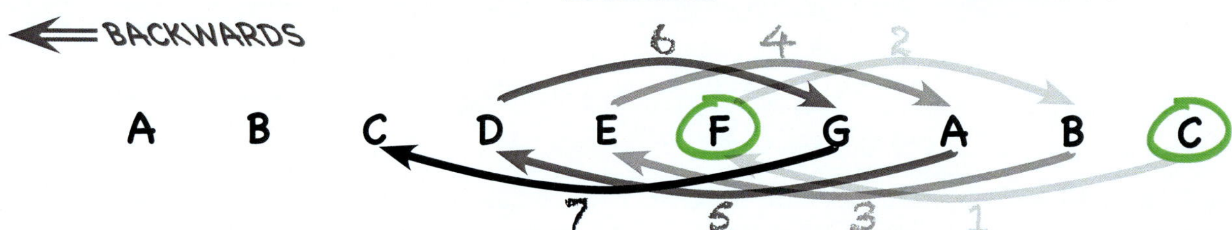

We ONLY need to remember B♭ and E♭ and alternate backward between the TWO to figure out the rest of the FLATS.

F♯ and C♯ are the first 2 sharps we learn on the violin so would be easy to remember.

NO.	FLATS	SCALE
0	-	C major
1	B♭	F major
2	B♭, E♭	B♭ major
3	B♭, E♭, A♭	E♭ major
4	B♭, E♭, A♭, D♭	A♭ major
5	B♭, E♭, A♭, D♭, G♭	D♭ major
6	B♭, E♭, A♭, D♭, G♭, C♭	G♭ major
7	B♭, E♭, A♭, D♭, G♭, C♭, F♭	C♭ major

We ONLY need to remember C and G and alternate backwards between the TWO to figure out the rest in order.

Add a flat on the scale onwards as without the flat, the scales would be scales that have sharps and not flats.

Same thing as figuring out the flats. All you have to remember is B♭ and E♭.
Then <u>alternate</u> them backward to figure out the rest.

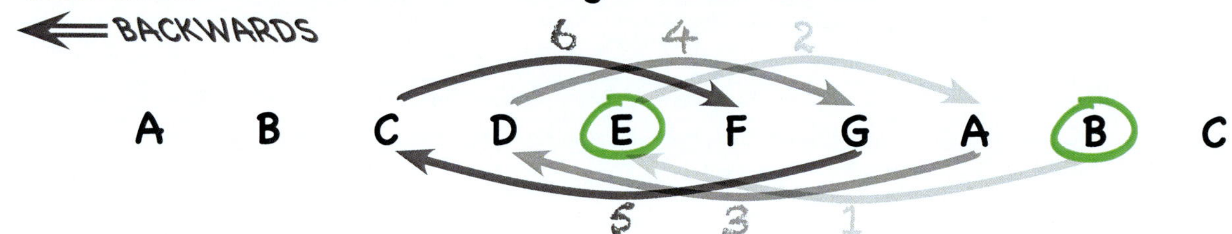

2. <u>Circle of fifths</u> (commonly used)

Refering to the diagram, C major is on top with no sharps or flats in its key signature. Each stop after 5 counts (eg. C to G is 5 counts, G to D is 5 counts, etc) on the circle as you go clockwise from C is a key with one sharp more than the previous key.

However, counting counter-clockwise from C (eg. C to F counting backwards) is a key with one flat more than the previous key.
Similarly for each scale, you identify the sharps by counting 5 forwards and flats by counting 5 backwards.

For example, F♯ to C♯ and C♯ to G♯ is 5 counts counting forwards,
B♭ to E♭ and E♭ to A♭ is 5 counts counting backwards.

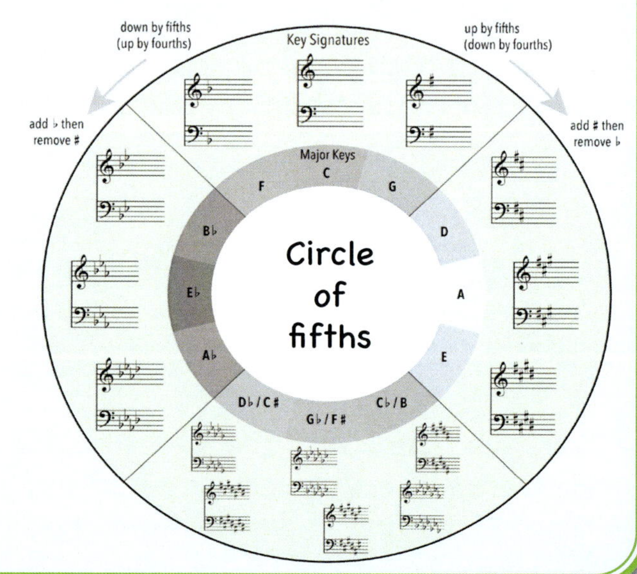

3. Using acronyms may also help memorize the sequence of the sharps and flats for each scale. See below for examples or try making up your own.

Fat **C**at **G**ives **D**ad **A**n **E**njoyable **B**agel. **(SHARPS)**

Before **E**ating **A** **D**onut **G**et **C**hocolate **F**irst. **(FLATS)**

1. Figure out the scales and their key signature on the table below.

NO.	SHARPS	SCALE
0		
1		
2		
3		
4		
5		
6		
7		

NO.	FLATS	SCALE
0		
1		
2		
3		
4		
5		
6		
7		

2. Answer the questions below.

a. Which scale has TWO flats in its key signature? _______________________________

b. Which scale has THREE sharps in its key signature? _______________________________

c. Which scale has NO flats or sharps in its key signature? _______________________________

d. Which scale has FIVE flats in its key signature? _______________________________

e. How many sharps does B major have? Name them. _______________________________

f. How many flats does Db major have? Name them. _______________________________

g. What key signature does E major have? _______________________________

The Sharp and Flat symbols are ALWAYS written in the same order as we can see from pages 31 to 33. These are how they would look on the stave.

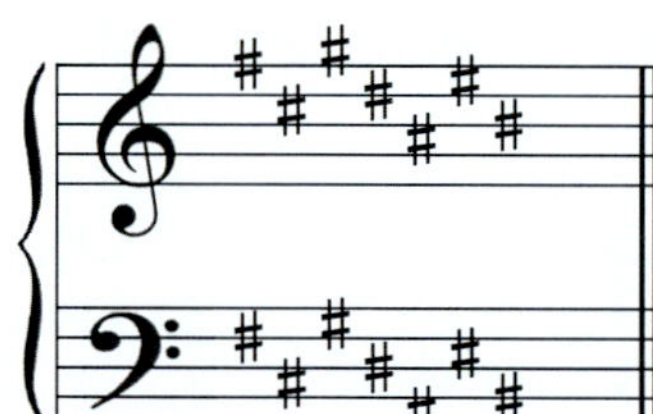

3. Draw all the sharps and flats on both clefs in the correct order. Do this without referring to the above.

So far we are able to work out the key of a piece of music by looking at the key signature. After learning minor scales, we know that the music could be in either a major key or its relative minor key.

Below are a few key points in being able to identify the key signature of a piece of music.

1. **Look at the key signature. How many flats or sharps are there?**
2. **Are there any accidentals?** (Yes? Then it's a minor.)
3. **Look at the first and the last note of the tune to confirm the key.**

(The note is usually the tonic note of the scale.)

4. Figure out the key of each of these tunes using the points above.

Key: _______________________________

Key: _______________________________

Key: _______________________________

Tonic Triad And Broken Chords

Let us look at the __tonic triad__ of the minor scales. Remember that the chord is made up of notes of an arpeggio of a scale.

(1st, 3rd, and 5th degree notes of the scale.)

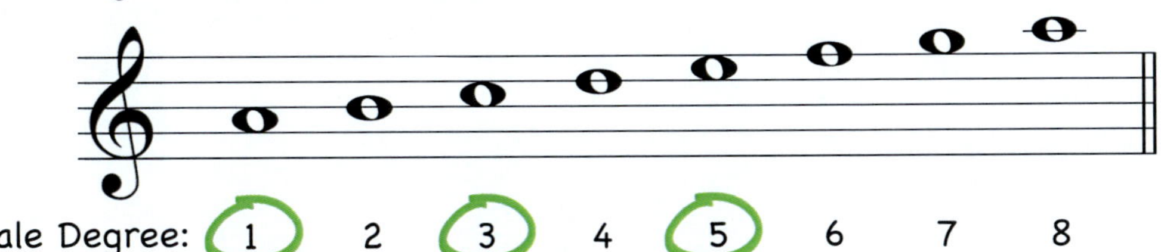

Scale Degree: 1   2   3   4   5   6   7   8

Below is how the tonic triad in the key of A minor is written.

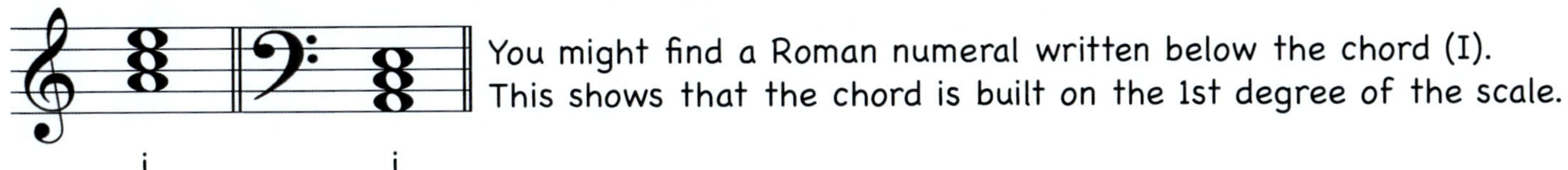

You might find a Roman numeral written below the chord (I).
This shows that the chord is built on the 1st degree of the scale.

As you know, we can also use letters to label our chords. For a minor chord, we use 'm' to identify them as minor chords.

Eg.

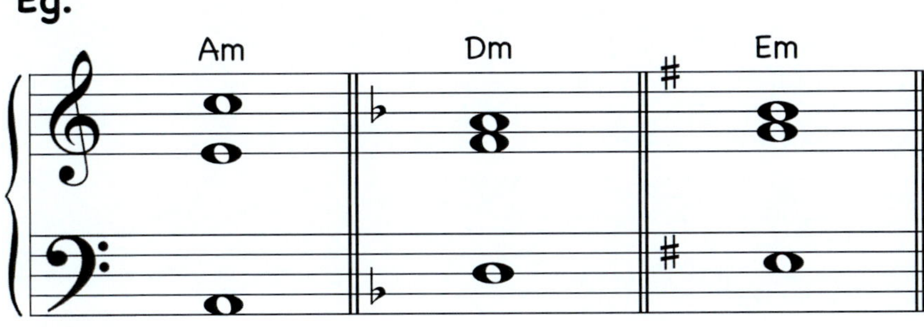

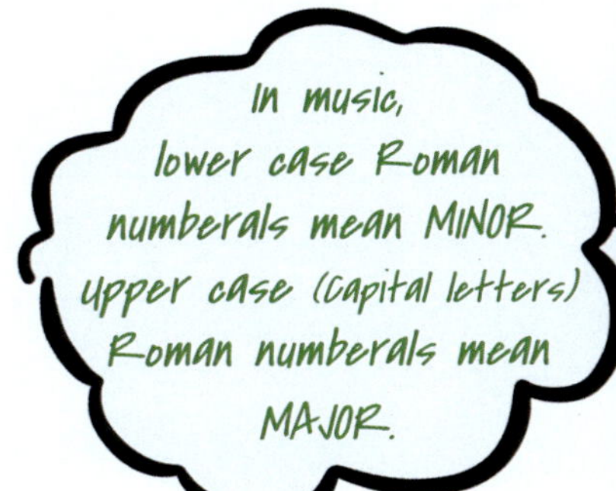

1. Add the missing notes of these tonic triads in the major and minor keys.

2. Write the key signature and tonic triad for each of the following keys.

3. The following music is written using notes from the tonic triads which we have already learnt. Name the key of the chord and label the chord using Roman numerals.

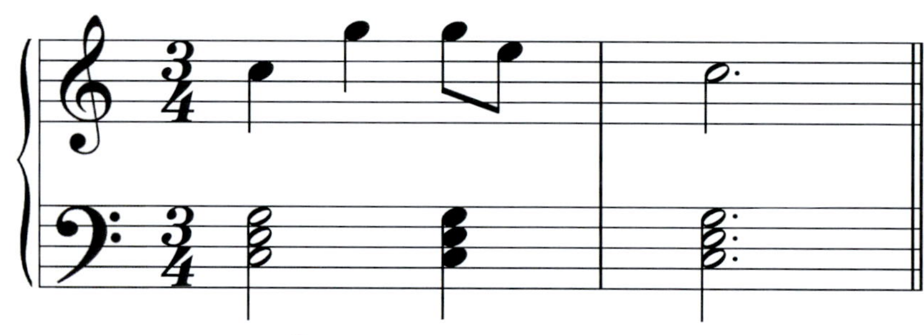

Key: _____ *C major* _____   Chord: _____ *I* _____

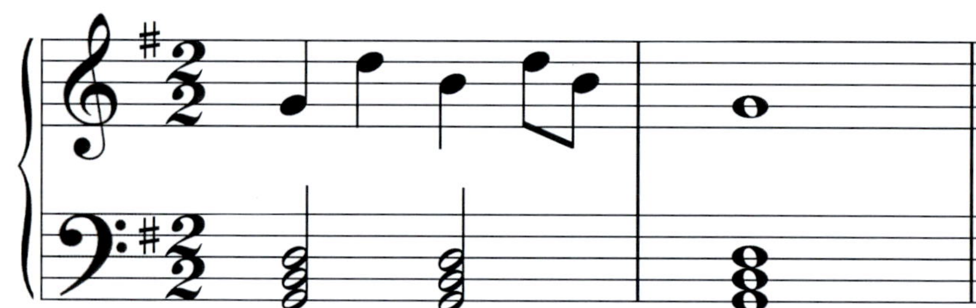

Key: _________________   Chord: _____________

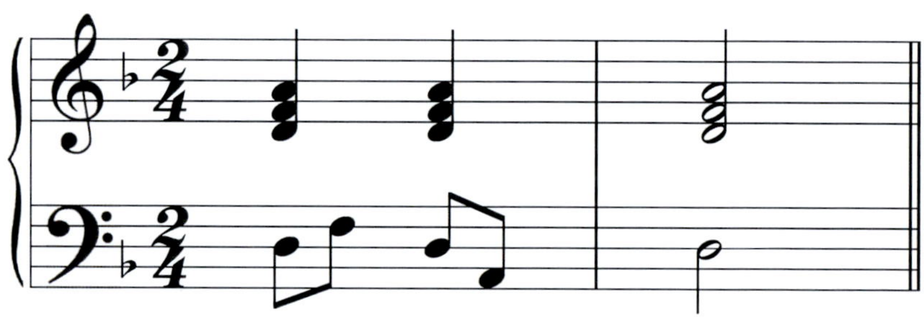

Key: _________________   Chord: _____________

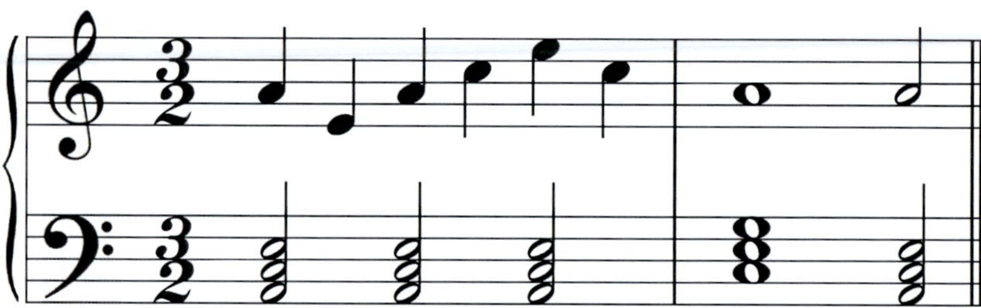

Key: _________________   Chord: _____________

Key: _________________   Chord: _____________

<u>Broken Chords</u> are like arpeggios made out of breaking up the chords in root position and its inversions.
There are a few ways in which we can write broken chords using different rhythmic patterns.

Below are some possible ways using the tonic triad of F major.

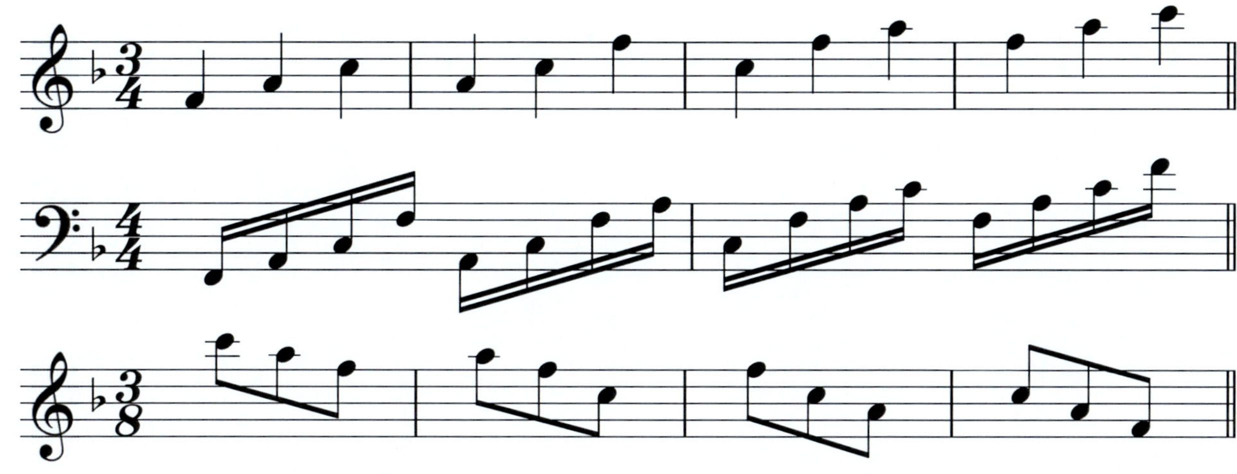

4. Using quavers beamed in fours, write a broken chord using G major tonic triad. Use patterns of four notes each time. Finish on the first G below the stave.

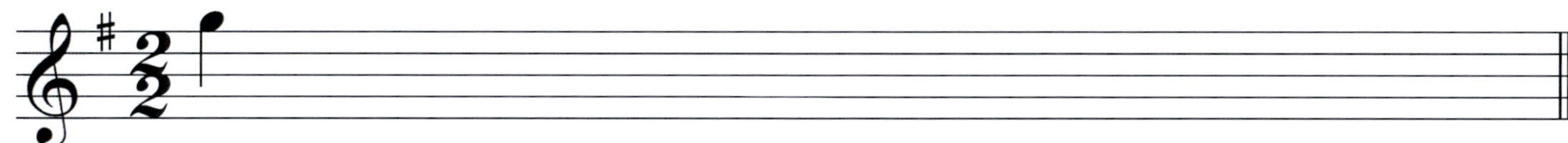

5. Using crotchets, write a broken chord using A minor tonic triad. Use patterns of four notes each time. Finish on the first E above the stave.

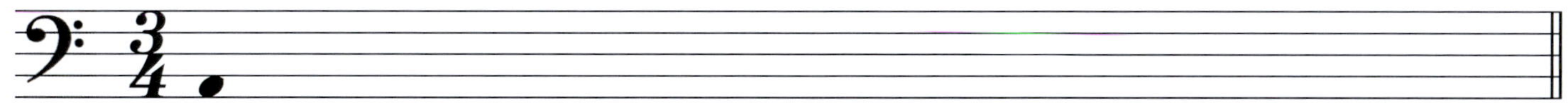

6. Using semiquavers beamed in fours, write a broken chord using D minor tonic triad. Use patterns of four notes each time. Finish on the first D below the stave.

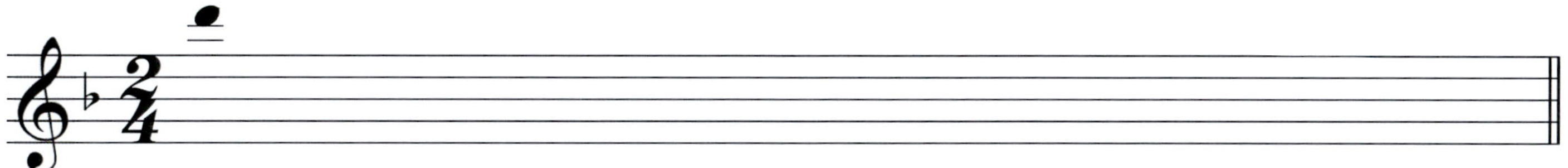

7. Using crotchets, write a broken chord using G major tonic triad. Use patterns of four notes each time. Finish on the first G above the stave.

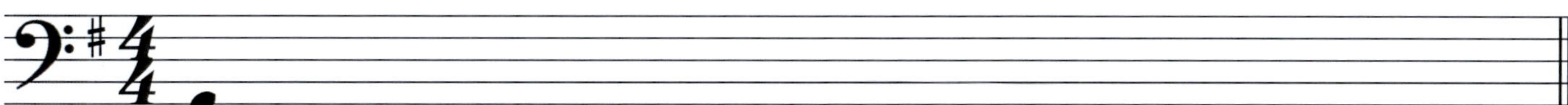

Sequence

A sequence is a melodic pattern that is repeated starting on a different note each time either moving the whole pattern upwards or downwards.

Eg.

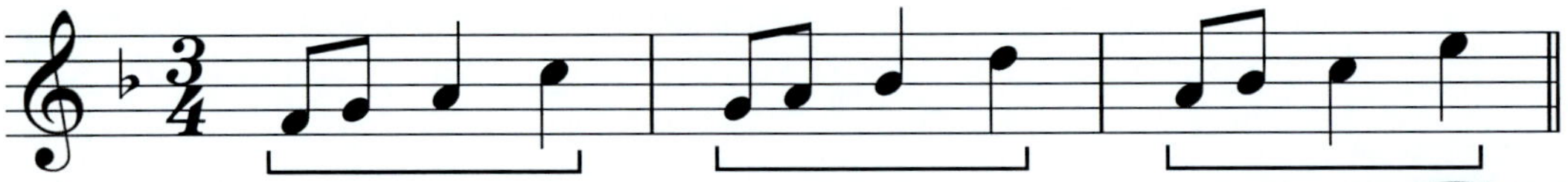

1. Draw a bracket (⌐¬) over each step of the sequence.

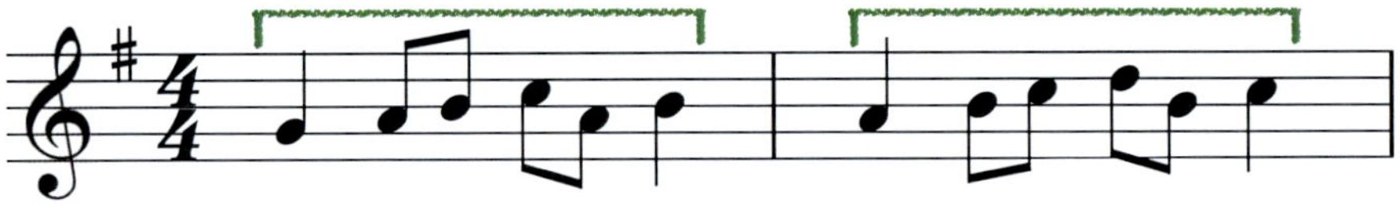

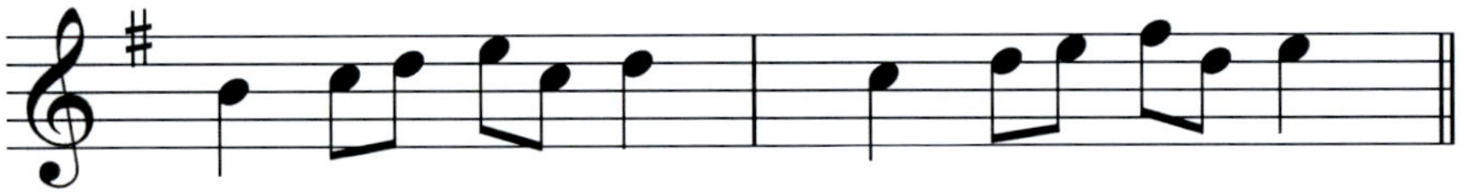

> Ostinato vs. Sequence
> Ostinato is a repeated rhythmic pattern with the same notes.
> Sequence is a repeated rhythmic and pitch pattern. It maintains the tune but moves the whole tune up or down.

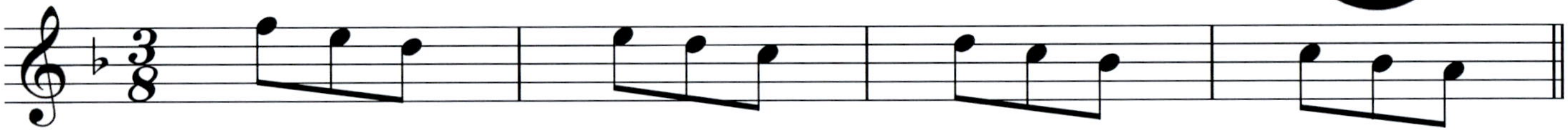

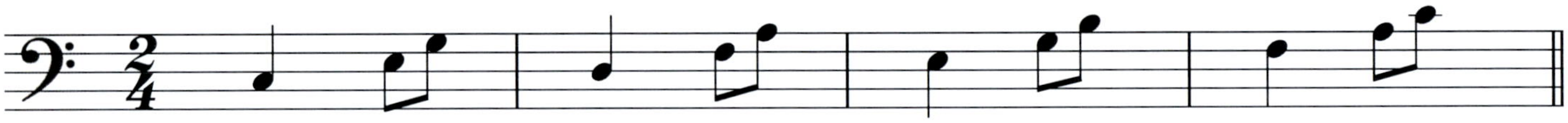

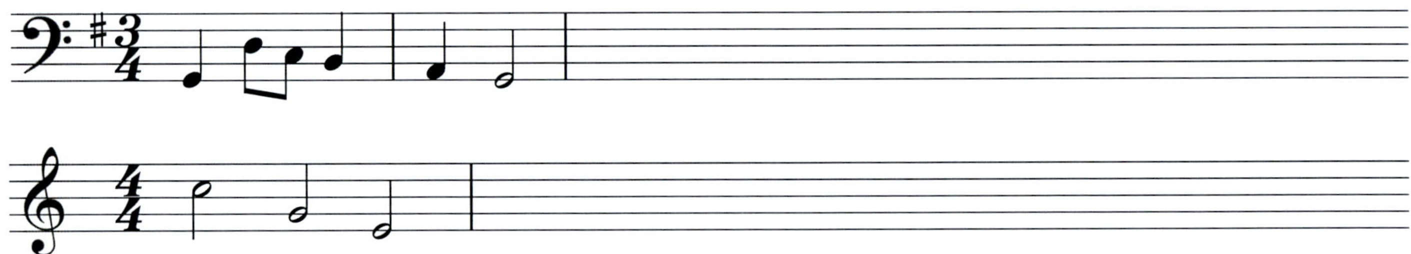

2. Make a sequence by repeating it twice, one note higher each time using the given tune.

3. Make a sequence by repeating it twice, one note lower each time using the given tune.

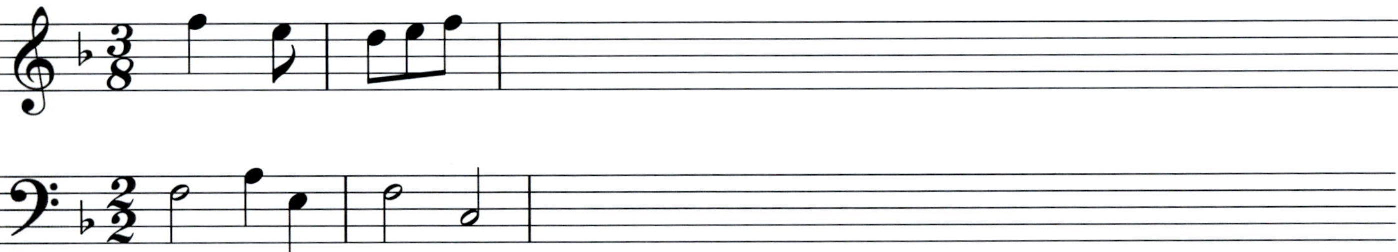

Intervals And Their Quality

In Grade 1, we learnt that an interval means the distance between two notes.
A reminder that it does not matter if you are reading from a treble or bass clef. To find an interval, count from the bottom note to the top.

In grade 2 you will need to identify the quality of the interval.
When the upper note is found in the major scale of the bottom note the interval is called **MAJOR** or **PERFECT**.

Look at these intervals below with the bottom note as the tonic D. The top of each interval comes from the D major scale. (D major has 2 sharps, F♯ and C♯.)

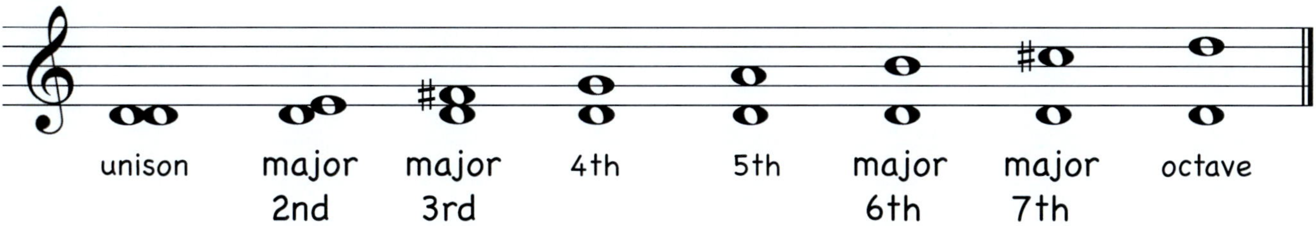

Unisons, 4ths, 5ths and octaves are exactly the same in any major or minor scale. Hence they are considered as PERFECT.

Now let us look at how we can identify the interval and its quality.

Name the bottom and the top note.

Eg.

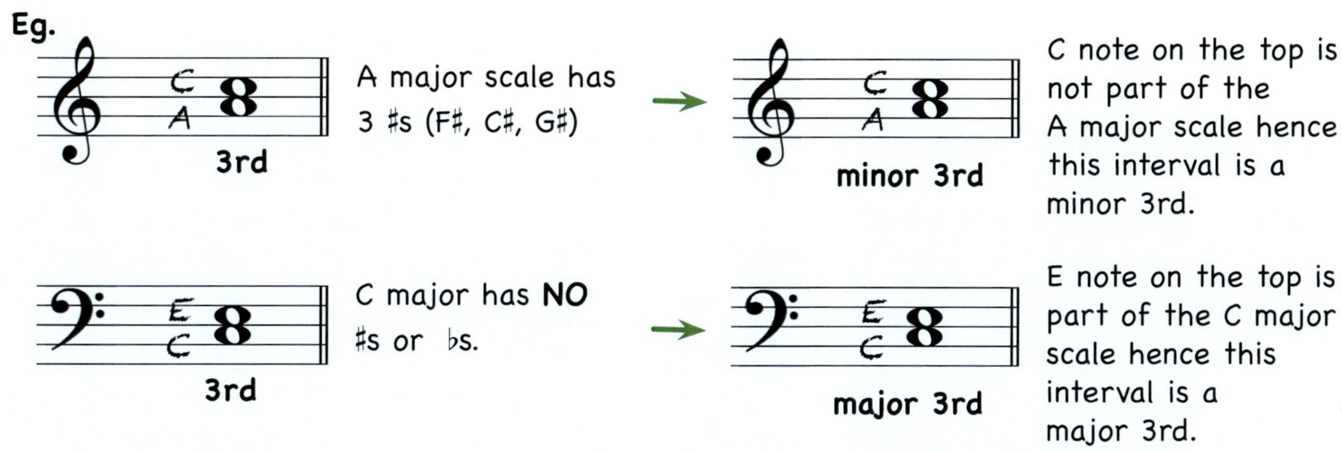

1. **Cross out the incorrect interval.**

1. careful of the clef. and *2. name the bottom and top note.*

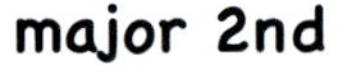

Eg.

major 3rd · major 2nd

perfect 5th · perfect 4th

minor 2nd · minor 3rd

2. **Name these intervals by number and quality.**

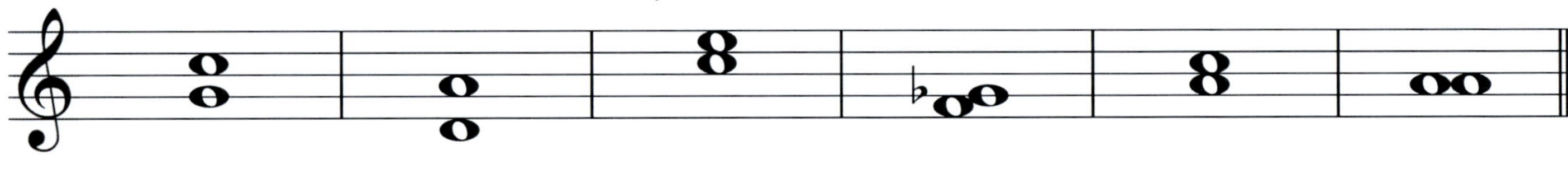

perfect 4th

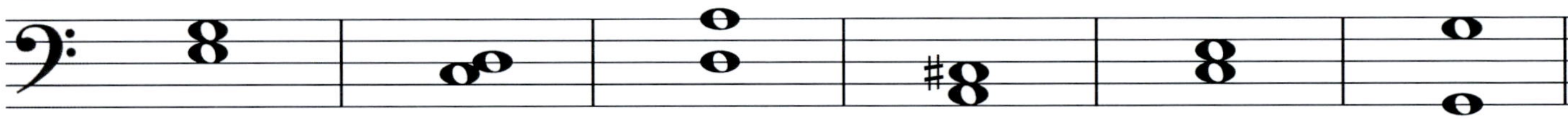

3. **In grade 2 we only work on 2nd, 3rd and perfect intervals. However for the curious mind, below are more intervals on 6ths and 7ths. Remember to name the notes and think of the key signatures of the appropriate scale.**

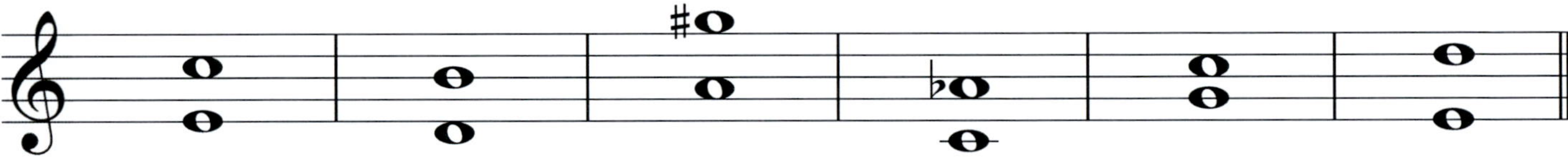

1st Inversion

Let us revise the major tonic triads which we have learnt in Grade 1.

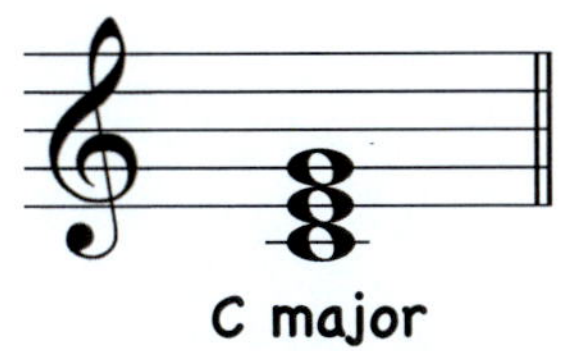
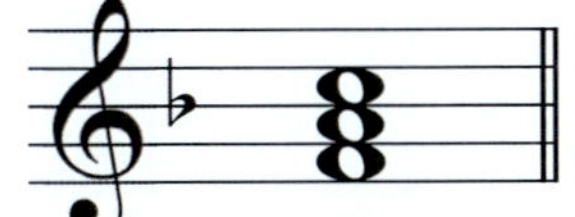

C major
tonic triad

F major
tonic triad

G major
tonic triad

The tonic triads above are called root position.
(The tonic note is at the bottom of the triad.)

The word inversion is when we invert the triad by taking the note which is at the bottom of the triad and place it up an octave.

Eg.

Here is a tonic triad in
C major in 1st inversion.

1st inversion: Only inverts 1 note from the bottom of the triad.

Write the tonic triad in root position of each key and then write its 1st inversion.
(Take care of the clefs.)

G major

Eg.

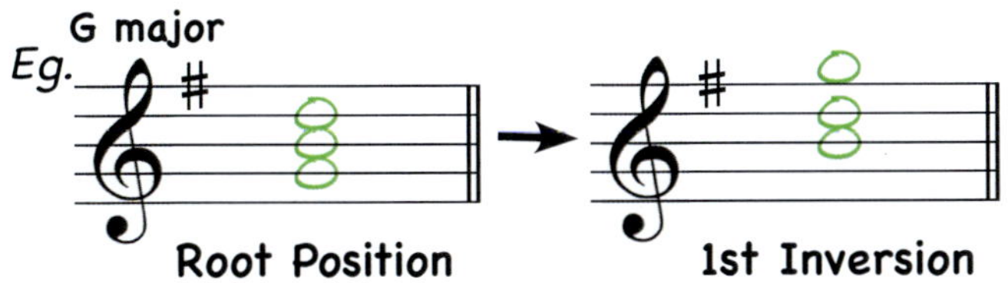

Root Position   1st Inversion

3.   E minor

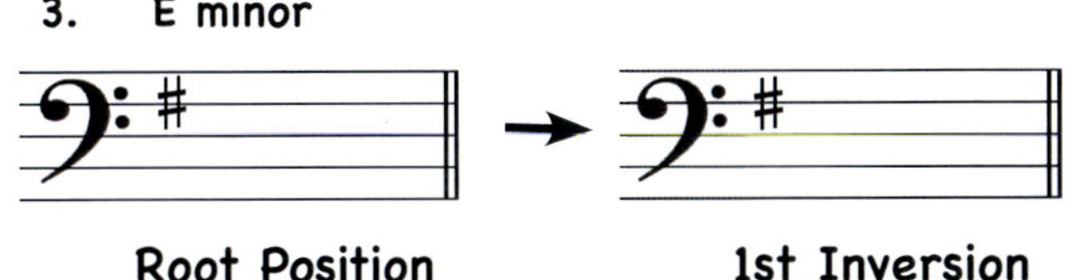

Root Position   1st Inversion

1.   D minor

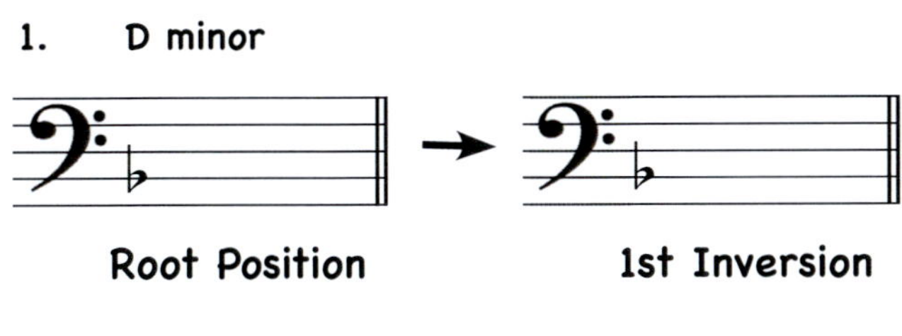

Root Position   1st Inversion

4.   F major

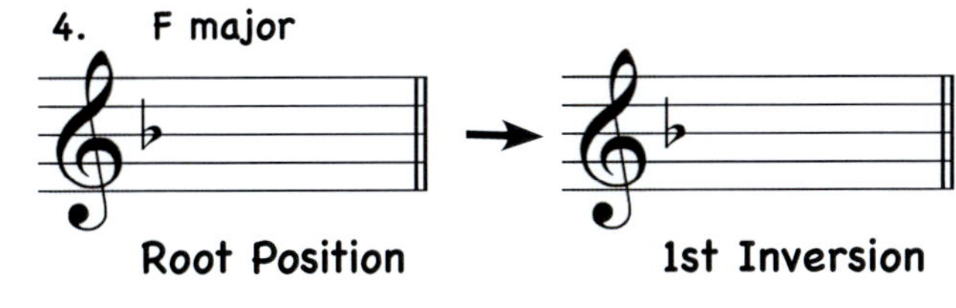

Root Position   1st Inversion

2.   A minor

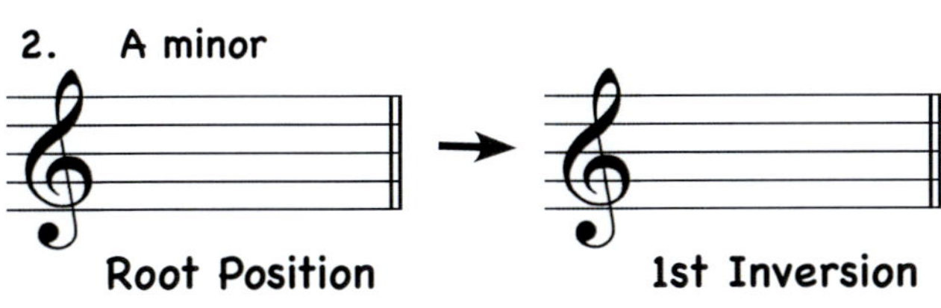

Root Position   1st Inversion

5.   C major

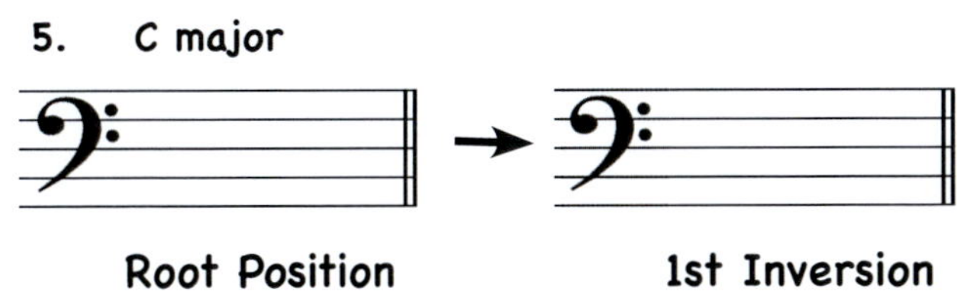

Root Position   1st Inversion

Transposition

Music transposition refers to moving a collection of notes up or down to different keys. We sometimes transpose music to suit a player's music range or to make it easier for the player to read the notes.

In Grade 2 we will only learn to transpose a tune up or down an octave.

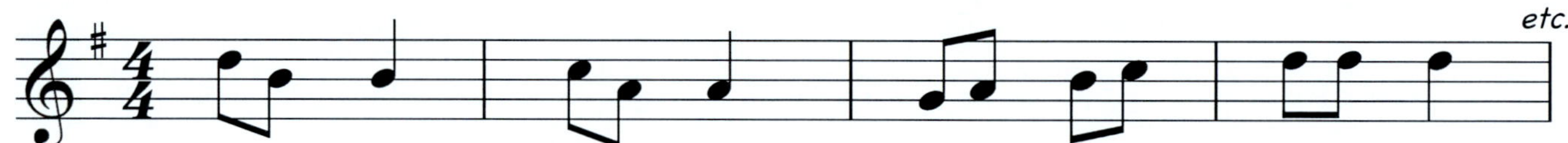

We will transpose the above melody an octave lower. First thing to do when transposing an octave is to name every note of the original melody.

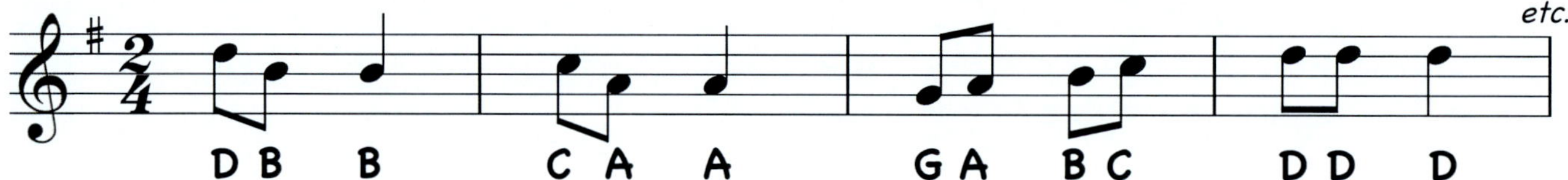

Now find the next note with the same letter name lower or higher to the first note and start writing from there. In this case find the same note but lower.

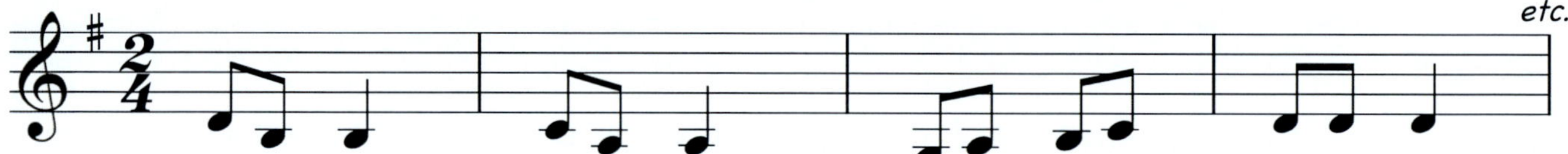

You can also do this task by following the note movement of the original tune.

1. Transpose these tunes down an octave.

Draw the clef, key signature and double bar lines.

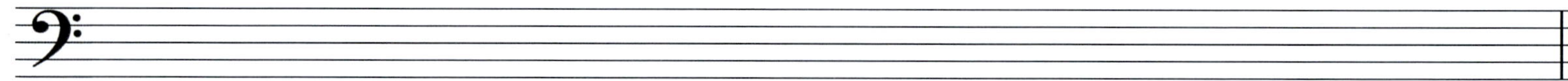

2. Transpose these tunes up an octave.

Draw the clef, key signature and double bar lines.

Composition

Song writing
There are many ways of creating and writing out a short tune.
First we start by creating a rhythm pattern to assist us.

End each rhythm with a long note.

1. Write 4 bar rhythms using the note and rest values which you have learnt. Include at least <u>THREE</u> rests in every rhythm.

More printable worksheets available on **www.stringstastic.com**

There are many ways of composing music. In Grade 1 we learnt how to create our own melody to a given rhythm.

In Grade 2, we learn how to write short tunes by using notes only from the tonic triad of a given scale.

Start and end the tune using the tonic note.

1. Write a tune using notes of the tonic triad to a given key and rhythm.
Eg. <u>G major</u>

The tonic triad for G major is **G B D.**
Below is one way we can write a tune using these notes.

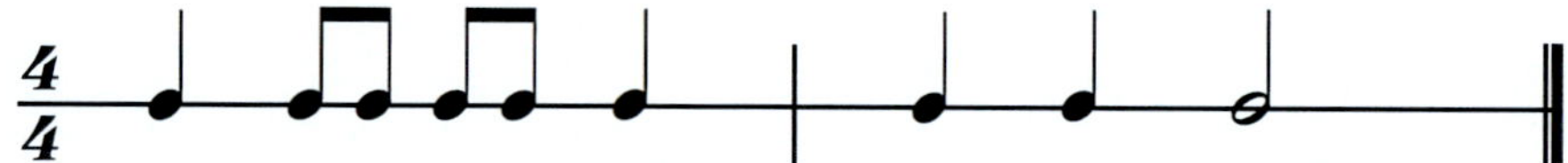

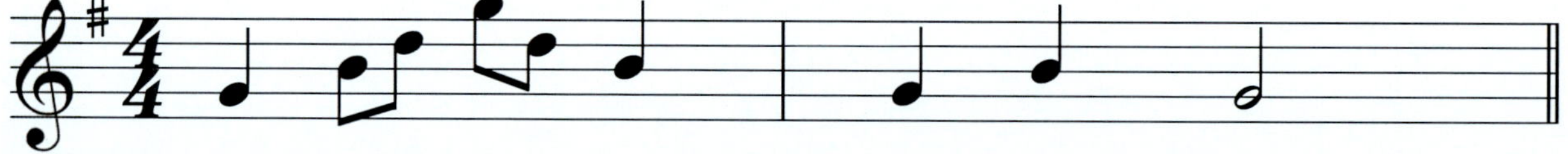

2. **Write a tune using notes of a tonic triad to the given scale and rhythm.**

Write in the key signature.

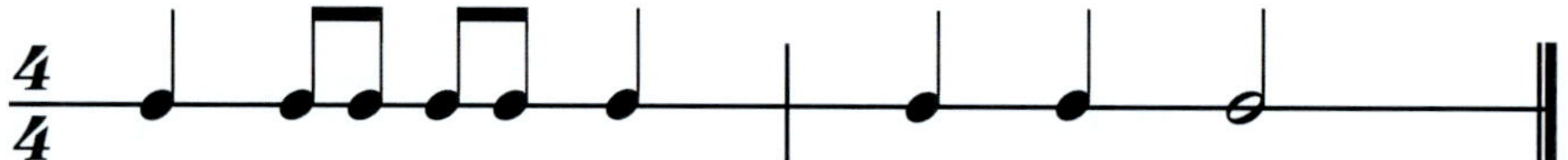

2. Write a tune using the first FIVE scale degrees (notes) to a given key and rhythm.

Eg. <u>D minor</u>

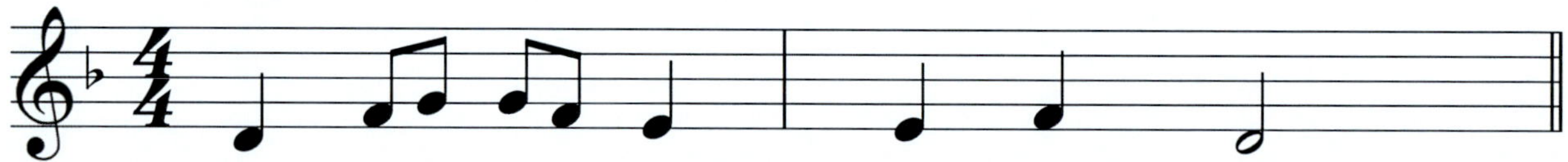

The first 5 notes for D minor are **D E F G A.**
Below is one way we can write a tune using these notes.

Start and end the tune using the tonic note.

3. Write a tune using the first FIVE notes of a given scale and rhythm.

A minor

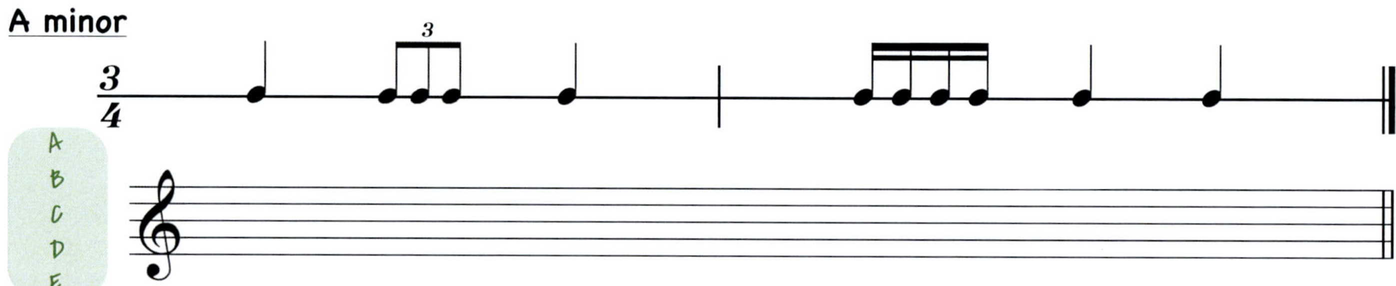

G major

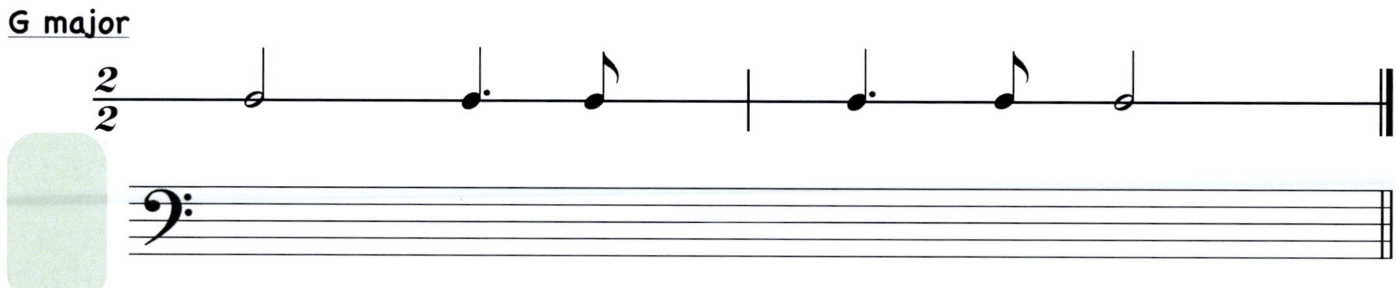

C major

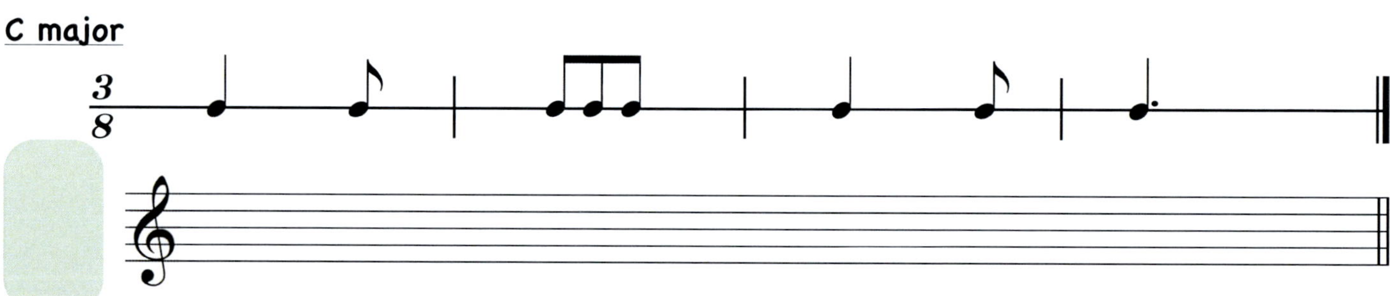

Now try playing these compositions which you have just written in question 1 and 2 in the treble clef on your violin.
Take care with the accidentals used. When do you lower your first and second finger in these short tunes?

www.stringstastic.com

Musical Words and Symbols

Tempo is the speed at which music is played. The tempo indication is usually placed above the music at the beginning of a piece.

1. Let us revise what we have learnt in Grade 1. Fill in the blank where needed.

Vivace or **Vivo** – fast and lively

Allegro – _______________________

Allegretto – moderately fast (but slower than Allegro)

Moderato – _______________________

Andante – _______________________

Adagio or **Lento** – slowly

mosso – movement

meno – less

piu – more

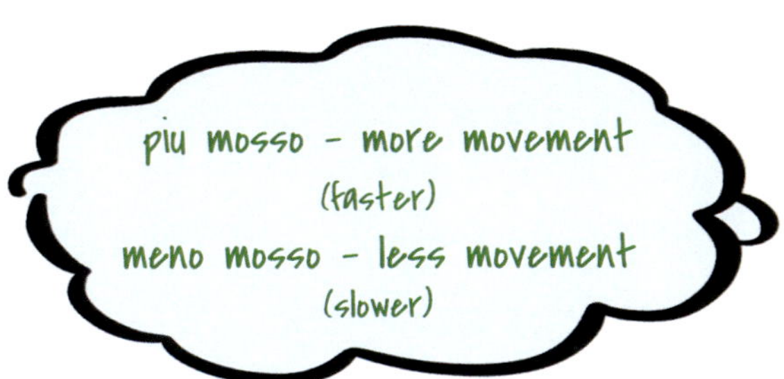

Some composers use metronome markings, M.M. (Maelzel's metronome) to give the exact speed of the beat. These markings tell the player how many quaver, crotchet or minim beats there are per minute.

Eg.

M.M. ♩ = 100   means 100 <u>crotchet</u> beats per minute

M.M. ♩ = 100   means 100 <u>minim</u> beats per minute

Most of the time M.M. is left out so that the marking is written as below.

Eg.   ♩ = 100

          ♩ = 100

2. Arrange the metronome markings in order.

The bigger the number, the faster it is.

♩ = 52

♩ = 100

♩ = 60

♩ = 112

♩ = 42

FASTEST

♩ = 112

SLOWEST

♩ = 52
♩ = 132
♩ = 48
♩ = 90
♩ = 120

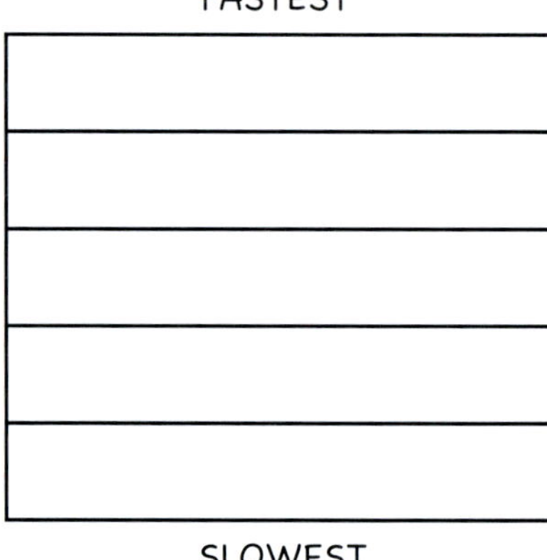

WHICH METRONOME MARKING IS FASTER?

♩ = 90
♪ = 120
♩ = 44
♩ = 72
♪ = 84

Change all the note values to the same beats. Either quaver, crotchet or minim beats. I have chosen crotchet beats.

Remember that quavers are smaller and minims are bigger then crotchets.

♩ = 90	♩ = 90
♪ = 120	♩ = 120 ÷ 2 = 60 *(divide numbers when changing quavers to crotchet)*
♩ = 44 ——→	♩ = 44 × 2 = 88 *(multiply numbers when changing minims to crotchet)*
♩ = 72	♩ = 72 × 2 = 144
♪ = 84	♩ = 84 ÷ 2 = 42

Hence,

♩ = 90
♪ = 120
♩ = 44
♩ = 72 **FASTEST** ✓
♪ = 84 (SLOWEST)

Try and remember this formula,

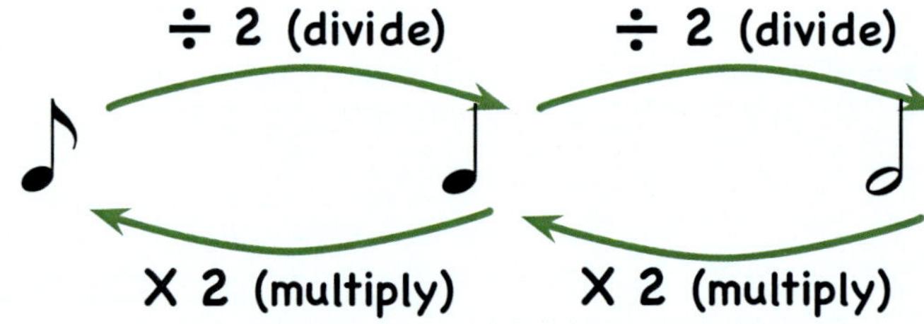

3. Arrange the metronome markings in order. *(Do your calculation on the right.)*

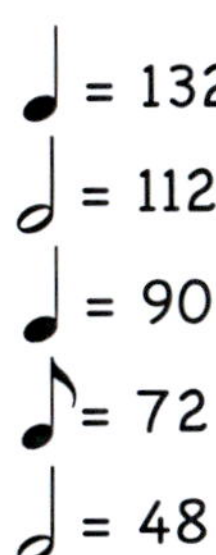

♩ = 52
♪ = 220
𝅗𝅥 = 90
♪ = 84
𝅗𝅥 = 72

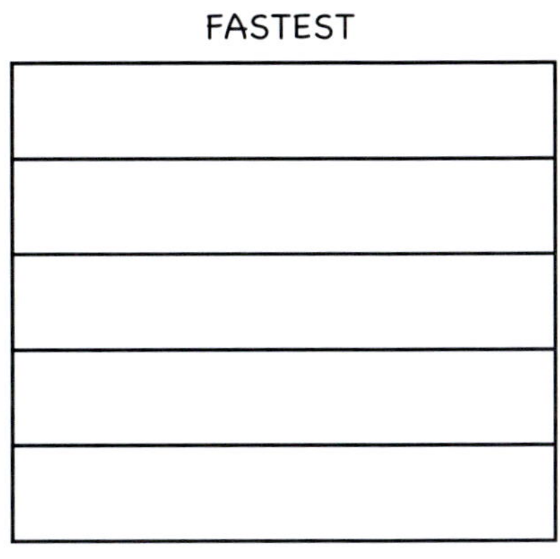

♩ = 132
𝅗𝅥 = 112
♩ = 90
♪ = 72
𝅗𝅥 = 48

FASTEST

SLOWEST

Expression Markings

Expression Marking tells a player in what kind of mood to play the music.
They are written below the music.

cantabile – in a singing style
maestoso – majestically
espressivo – expressively
grazioso – gracefully
dolce – sweetly
*fortissimo (**ff**)* – VERY loud
*pianissimo (**pp**)* – VERY soft

Other Markings

Expression Marking tells a player in what kind of mood to play the music.
They are written below the music.

allargando – becoming broader
largo – broadly
leggiero – lightly
sempre – always
senza – wihout
sostenuto – sustained
molto – very

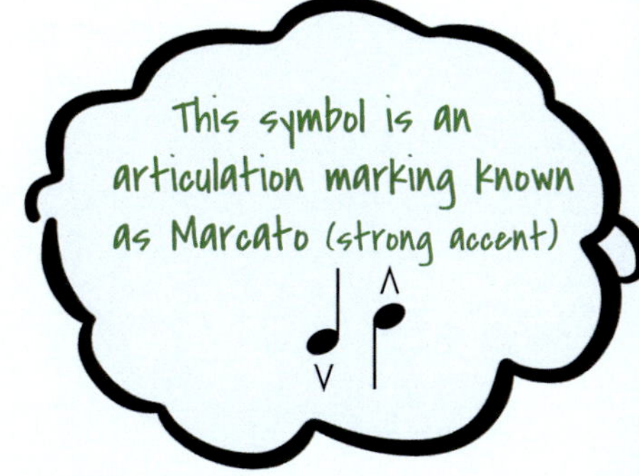

Sometimes the way we remember meanings of terms is by looking at the first few letters of the music term. It is usually close to the english definition.

4. Show that this piece is played in a moderate speed. Add dynamic markings to show that it should be played moderately loud. Add tenuto signs to all the minims and add a phrase mark to show that this music is to be played as one phrase. There should also be a pause on the last note.

5. Show that this music is played very expressively. It should be played in a walking speed and slows down from the last note of bar 3. It should also be played loudly. Add a phrase mark to show that this music is to be played as one phrase.

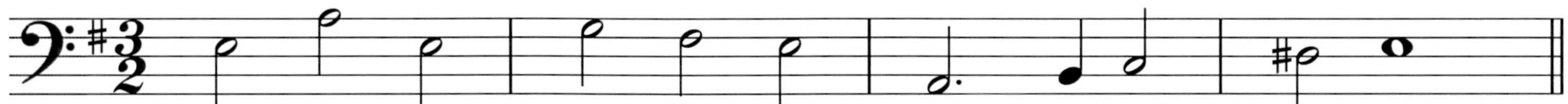

6. Show that this music is played slowly and in a singing style. Add an accent on the first note of each bar. The music should be played loudly. It should be an octave lower than written. Add a slur on the repeated rhythmic sections to show that the music has TWO phrases.

7. Show that this music is played quite fast. Add dynamic markings to show that it should be played moderately loud. Accent the first minim of each bar and the crotchet notes should be slurred in pairs.

8. Show that this music is played gracefully. It should be played in a moderate speed and an octave lower than written. This tune should be played moderately soft. Add staccato markings on all the crotchets except the last note which should have a pause written on top of it. Show that this music is played as one phrase.

Analysis

1. **Look at the following piece and answer the questions below. Only some of the answers are given.**

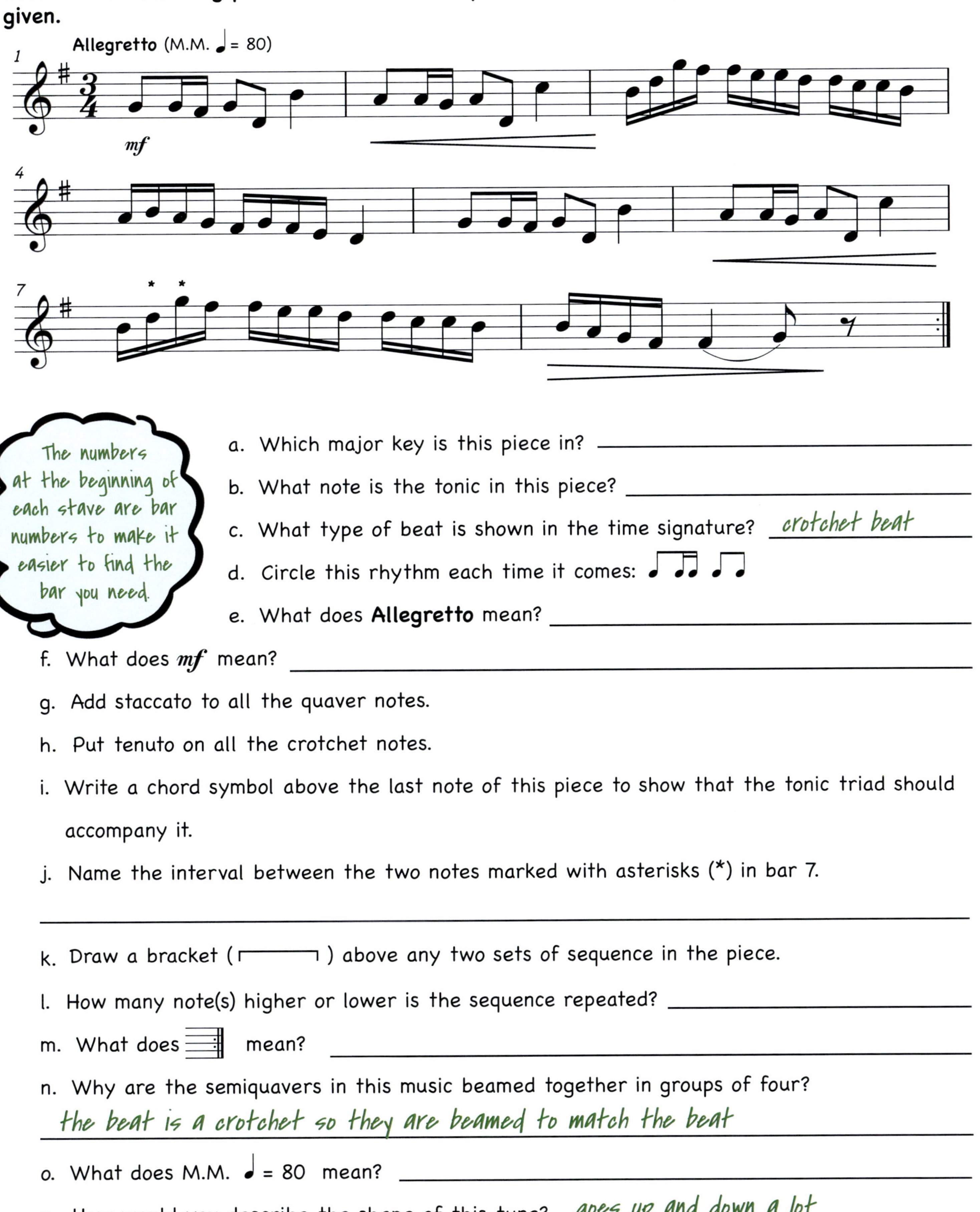

a. Which major key is this piece in? _______________________

b. What note is the tonic in this piece? _______________________

c. What type of beat is shown in the time signature? *crotchet beat*

d. Circle this rhythm each time it comes: ♩ ♫ ♫ ♩ ♫

e. What does **Allegretto** mean? _______________________

f. What does *mf* mean? _______________________

g. Add staccato to all the quaver notes.

h. Put tenuto on all the crotchet notes.

i. Write a chord symbol above the last note of this piece to show that the tonic triad should accompany it.

j. Name the interval between the two notes marked with asterisks (*) in bar 7.

____

k. Draw a bracket (⌐‾‾‾¬) above any two sets of sequence in the piece.

l. How many note(s) higher or lower is the sequence repeated? _______________________

m. What does 𝄇 mean? _______________________

n. Why are the semiquavers in this music beamed together in groups of four?
   the beat is a crotchet so they are beamed to match the beat

o. What does M.M. ♩ = 80 mean? _______________________

p. How would you describe the shape of this tune? *goes up and down a lot*

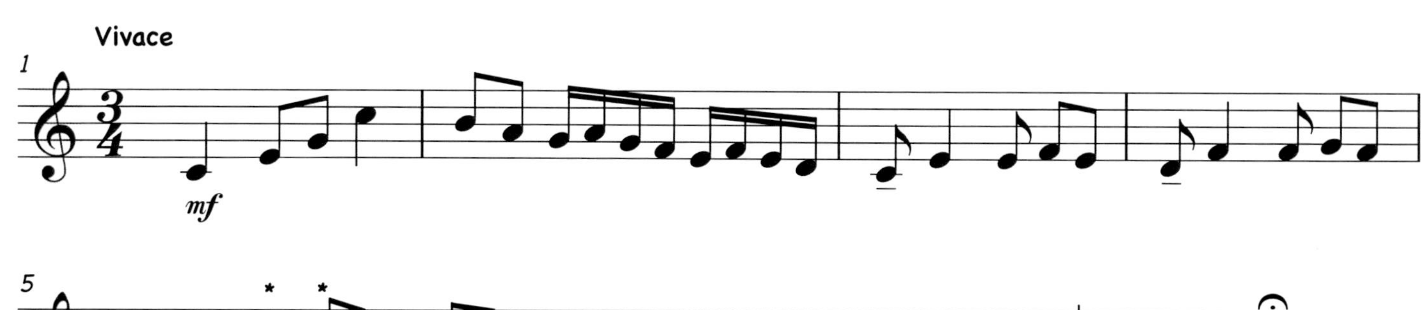

a. Which major key is this piece in? ____

b. What note is the tonic in this piece? ____

c. What type of beat is shown in the time signature? ____

d. Circle this rhythm each time it comes:

e. Draw a bracket (⌐⎯⎯⎯⌐) above a sequence in bar 3 and 4.

f. What is the musical word that describes the rhythm pattern that you have circled in

    question d.? ____

g. How many notes higher or lower is the sequence in bar 4 repeated?

____

h. What does **Vivace** mean? ____

i. How many tenuto notes are there in this piece? ____

j. How do you play a tenuto note? ____

k. In which bar is there a one octave ascending arpeggio? ____

l. Write a Roman numeral below the last note of this piece to show that the tonic triad

    should accompny it.

m. Name the interval between the two notes marked with asterisks (*) in bar 5.

____

n. Explain the differences and/or similarities between bar 2 and bar 6. _________________________

____

o. Name the highest and lowest notes of the piece? ____

p. What does ⌢ in bar 8 mean? ____

q. How would you describe the shape of this tune? ____

a. Which key is this piece in? ______________________________

b. What note is the tonic in this piece? ______________________________

c. What type of beat is shown in the time signature? ______________________________

d. Circle this rhythm each time it comes:

e. Draw a bracket (⌐‾‾‾¬) above a sequence in bars 5 to 7.

f. What is the musical word that describes the rhythmic pattern in bars 5 to 7?

____

g. How many notes higher or lower is the sequence repeated?

____

h. Name the note with an accidental in bar 3. ______________________________

i. What does *mf* mean? ______________________________

j. How many phrases are there in this piece? ______________________________

k. What is the length of the rest in bar 4? ______________________________

l. Write a Roman numeral below the last note of this piece to show that the tonic triad should accompny it.

m. Name the interval between the two notes marked with asterisks (*) in bar 1.

____

n. What does molto espressivo mean? ______________________________

o. Name the highest and lowest notes of the piece? ______________________________

p. What does M.M. ♩ = 108 mean? ______________________________

Revision

1. Add the total number of crotchet beats of silence in these rests.

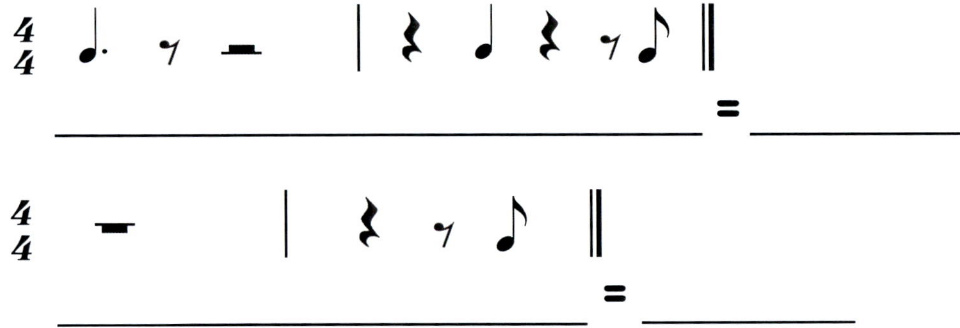

__________________________ = ______

____________________ = ______

2. The following table contains incorrect note and rest groupings. Correct them without swapping any notes or rests, maintaining the rhythm of each bar.

INCORRECT ✗	CORRECT ✓
$\frac{3}{4}$ ♩ ▬	♩ 𝄽 𝄽
$\frac{4}{4}$ ♫ ♫♫ ♫	
$\frac{3}{2}$ ♩ ▬ 𝄽 ♩	
$\frac{3}{8}$ ♪ ♪ ♪	
¢ ▬	
$\frac{2}{4}$ ♪ 𝄽 𝄾	
$\frac{2}{2}$ ♩ ▬ ♩	
$\frac{3}{4}$ ♩. 𝄽 ♪	
¢ ♩♩♩ 𝄽 ♫	
$\frac{3}{2}$ ♩. 𝄽 ♪𝄾𝄾♩	
$\frac{4}{4}$ ♪ ♪ ♩ ▬	

3. Write a 4 bar rhythm using the note and rest values which you have learnt. Include at least __THREE__ rests in every rhythm.

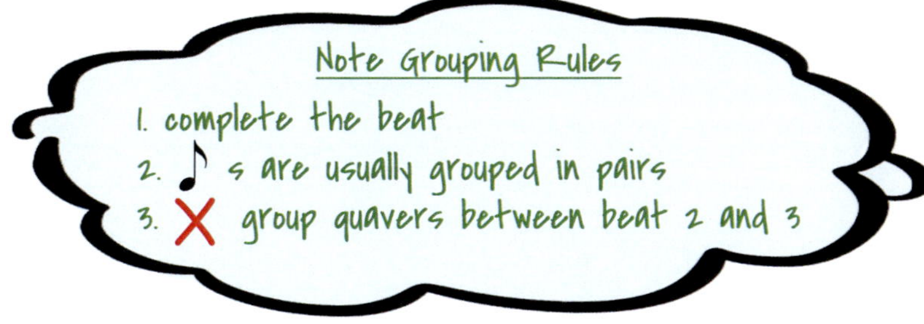

$\dfrac{3}{2}$

$\dfrac{3}{4}$

$\dfrac{4}{4}$

$\dfrac{3}{8}$

$\dfrac{2}{4}$

𝄴

$\dfrac{2}{2}$

4. What is the relative minor scale for G major? ________________________________

5. What is the relative major scale for A minor? ________________________________

6. Which scale has TWO flats in its key signature? ________________________________

7. Which scale has THREE sharps in its key signature? ________________________________

8. What does *cantabile* mean? ________________________________

9. What does *molto grazioso* mean? ________________________________

10. **Write a tune using notes of the tonic triad of G major to these given rhythms below.**

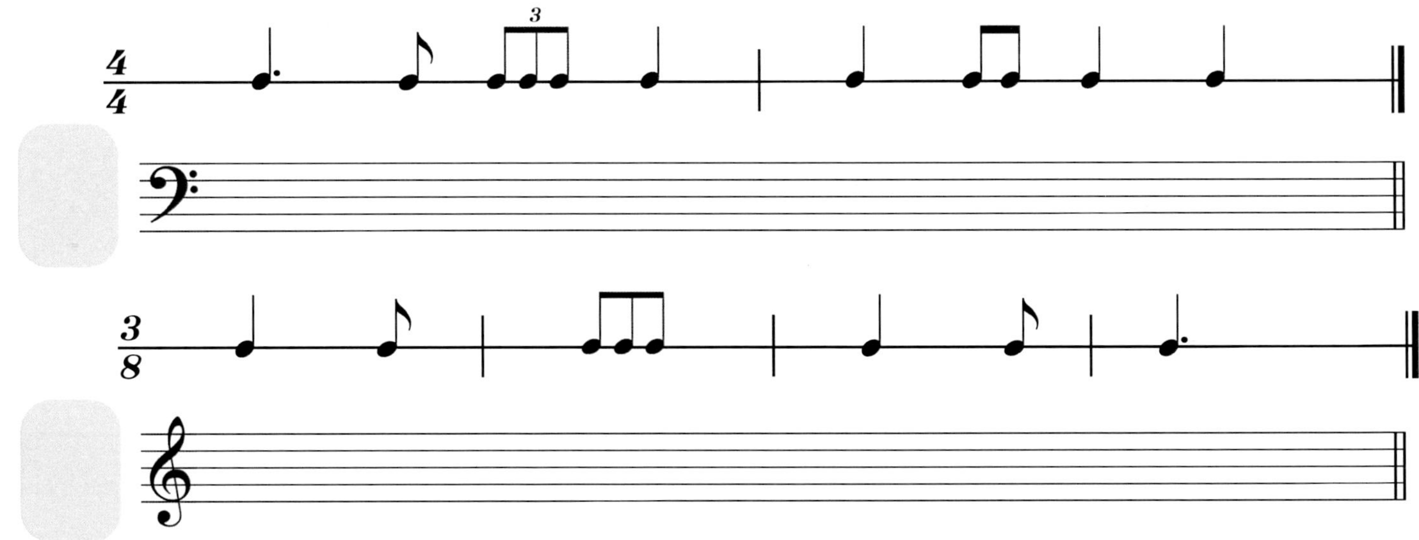

11. **Using the same rhythm above, write a tune using the first FIVE notes of the same scale.**

12. **Look at the following music. Add the time signature and bar lines accordingly.**